# TRY BEING HEALTHY

by
Alec Forbes
MA.,DM(Oxon).F.R.C.P.(London)

LANGDON BOOKS
The Old Laundry
Langdon, Wembury, Plymouth

*By the same author*
Try Being Human

© H.A.W. Forbes 1976

ISBN 0 850 321 409

Printed by Whitstable Litho Ltd.
Whitstable
Kent

# TRY BEING HEALTHY

## CONTENTS

| | | Page |
|---|---|---|
| Preface | | 1 |
| 1 | A Time for Change | 4 |
| 2 | Acupuncture | 14 |
| 3 | Allopathy (Medicine) | 19 |
| 4 | Anthroposophical Therapy | 24 |
| 5 | Body Dynamics – Chiropractic, Osteopathy, Alexander Technique, Rolfing, Hatha Yoga, T'ai Chi | 32 |
| 6 | Healing | 43 |
| 7 | Herbalism | 53 |
| 8 | Homoeopathy | 58 |
| 9 | Miscellaneous – Bach Remedies, Biofeedback, Colour and Gem Therapy, Cymatics, Magnetism, Orgone, Vita Florum | 66 |
| 10 | Naturopathy | 92 |
| 11 | Oriental Therapy – History, Ayurveda, Far Eastern Therapy, Tibetan Therapy | 96 |
| 12 | Psychology – Psychiatry, Psychotherapy, Hypnosis, Autosuggestion, Autogenic Training, Christian Science, Meditation | 122 |
| 13 | Radiesthesia including Radionics and Psionic "Medicine" | 135 |
| 14 | Tactical Solutions | 141 |
| 15 | The Strategy of Life | 152 |
| Bibliography and References | | 172 |
| Index | | 185 |

# Preface

In this book I am holding to the point of view which finds an underlying unity in everything, which considers all alternatives have meaning, and that their understanding leads to a new position. Everything is relative and subject to change in this, or any other world. A search for certainty is an illusory activity. The only stable, rigid certainty is death. Life is eternal, ever changing.

The public dictate the sort of therapy they think they want, and impose their ideas of health standards upon their therapists rather than the other way about. However, since each therapist is not only a member of the public, but also a unique individual, each of them has his own idea of the role he has to play. In the resulting chaotic situation I have tried to look at the scene as a man from outer space, from a civilisation with a more effective, less destructive technology than exists at present on earth, but who is well informed on present methods of therapy, and have endeavoured to help everyone to discover what he should be doing.

Only the briefest mention has been made of the supraphysical bodies of man, and none of the chakras. However, those who understand about these will be able to relate their knowledge readily to the text. I have selected current widely applicable systems of therapy which seem effective and illustrate a growing point, or a different principle from other methods, and hope that the underlying relationship between many of the systems will be seen, for I have tried to bring this out wherever possible. Inevitably the nature of health and the significance of life on earth have also been considered.

Many methods such as:— Aroma Therapy, Zone Therapy, Impact Therapy, Exaltation of Flowers and Manark Preparations, Iris and Hand Diagnosis, Alchemy, the Pyonex Treatment, African Witch Doctoring, Schussler's Salts, Megavitamin Therapy, Unani, American and Mexican Indian methods of healing have been omitted, but not because they are ineffective. Some are either too narrow in their field of application, or their mode of action is embraced by one or more systems described in this book. Others can only be understood by living in close relationship with their practitioners and gaining their confidence. With them, alas barriers of language, space and time prevent their inclusion at present.

Scientists and Registered Medical Practitioners will find that in order to understand how many of the systems work, they should stop thinking only in terms of the chemistry, atomic structures and electro-magnetic fields they already know about. They should not abandon these concepts, but open their minds to realise that there are also many levels of manifestation, many forms of vibration and energy fields that we do not know about yet, but which nevertheless govern our minds and bodies. We need a new science, a new Post-Einstein Theory of Relativity, a new Theory of Time, a new Model of the Universe.

It should be realised that the information gathered by the use of the experimental method is restricted by the horizons of those that use it. The limitations of individuals do not justify confining the application of the experimental method only to what can be explained by current knowledge and choosing to call it "Science". If a phenomenon cannot be explained this is all the more reason for trying to explain it by using the most rigorous experimental techniques that are available.

It is not my intention to imply that the Allopathic system of medicine, in which I was trained and willingly practice, is obsolescent. It will always be needed. Nevertheless, each system of therapy has inherent disadvantages when forced to encompass the treatment of every human disorder, unless it is also a way of life.

A lot of references have been given, in spite of the fact that the numbers used to indicate them tend to slow the flow of reading, in order to show that many people have thought as long as written records exist and are thinking today, on the lines discussed in this book. Some references are in heavy type, these have been selected to form a small bibliography for further reading.

I give my thanks to all my friends and colleagues in the Healing Art, especially to those practising the non medically registered systems, who have willingly informed me about their methods and corrected my mistakes; also to their patients who have described the ways in which they improved, as well as comparing various methods of treatment. If any errors remain they are my responsibility.

Plymouth, January, 1976

## CHAPTER 1

# A Time for Change

The minority systems of therapy have an uncertain future. They face the possibility of being outlawed by legislation supported by the Medical Practitioners in the EEC. Yet the system called Allopathy, or Medicine, which holds a dominant position in the Westernised world, is also suffering from harsh treatment.

In the past year there have been two major attacks on the medical system both from outside the profession. The first was by Ivan Illich, and the second by Rick Carlson, a lawyer, in an introduction to the book on the May lectures which took place in London in May 1974[32]. These were talks from serious researchers and doctors who wish to expand the frontiers of our present scientific and medical concepts. The title of Carlson's introduction, *The End of Medicine and the Beginning of Health* gives the gist of what he and others say in the book. Peter Blythe, a psychologist, also discussed these problems in 1974[23].

Criticism of the medical system even from within the profession has not been lacking from earlier times. Paracelsus and Hahnemann have been notable examples, and in 1898 Dr. Franz Hartmann wrote,

" . . . modern medical science has become degraded almost

into a mere trade flourishing under the protection of its self interests which it receives from governments. The medicine of the ancients was a holy art, requiring no artificial protection, because, standing on its own merit it rested on its own success". This is so relevant for the present that it strikes home keenly[80].

Ivan Illich in *Medical Nemesis* points out that the effect of Medicine on the death rate is negligible. The death rate responds to better living conditions, not Medicine; and the poisonings which Medicine itself produces (iatrogenic diseases), euphemistically called side effects, more than compensate for its successes. Illich, whose documentation of supporting evidence is impressive, says that the medical system also paralyses the individual's ability to respond to his difficulties[95].

However his solution is political. He suggests the disestablishment of Medicine, and says that "only a political programme aimed at the limitation of professional medicine enables people to recover their powers of self care". This seems to be Illich's weakest idea; since Political Hubris breeds Political Nemesis, just as much as he shows Medical Hubris to foster Medical Nemesis, it would be more useful to point out how to avoid hubris itself.

It would be better if each individual took responsibility for himself and, changing the quality of his life, finally realised that though each of us is unique, we are also all one. This is the only way that a collective solution can come about. In the exact formulation of a problem is its solution. When an individual sees exactly where his apparent difficulty lies — what in himself he needs to change — if he fully accepts that insight, change automatically occurs and there is no problem. If all people, or even more people, took this approach there would be far less need for the services of those who fix, or feel they ought to fix, man's ills.

Yet people do not do this, they have an innate tendency to organise. This allows the passive to shelve their responsibilities as individuals; the dependent to belong and satisfy the longing they have to possess an identity; the active to feel a sense of purpose; and the dominant to have a sense of power. So organisations are extremely popular. Like Frankenstein's Monster they take on an independent life of their own.

Formed initially to protect an interest of a group of like minded people on a small scale, or of a nation on a large scale, an organisation starts with a dogma which is immediately codified into rules or laws. Conceived in fear, as it grows its members feel secure. The negative emotion fear swings to its opposite, the desire to impose, and the organisation tries to convert others to its way of thinking and expand. On a national scale this often leads to war. Professions, business combines and evangelism are other examples[53].

In a mixed population, the majority of whom are less well behaved than animals, organisation is essential. A stable society would otherwise be impossible. However, successful organisations make decisions favourable to the interests of their leaders, establishments, governments, directors and executive committees. So long as they are alright the public don't really matter.

Illich illustrates this with examples from the field of health organisations and medicine. Sir Richard Acland does the same about Big Business in *The Next Step*[1]. Unlike Illich he does point out that an individual change is necessary first. It seems abundantly clear that the main effort required of mankind must be to become human in greater numbers and not proliferate organisations, which sap and coagulate the energy available for individual evolution[54].

Before he can conduct a long term strategy of life a man must deal first with his personality. He must find out why it is always getting him into difficulties. What is there about the personality that leads it into difficulties again and again — that produces the absurd society in which we live — with starvation in one country and a mortality from excessive food consumption in another — private squalor in the midst of public splendour — emotional disturbance in the home, with an orderly placid outward life — a feverish search for health and life at any price, except that of inner change?

## The Jack Principle

The key to the power house of the human personality is the Jack Principle. It has been variably expressed here and there for years, some times in coarse words. Here it is. Man's personality works on the principle of —

### SO LONG AS I'M ALRIGHT JACK

This is not a joke — it is deadly serious. Because of this principle practically everyone wants to avoid death, discomfort and unhappiness at any cost and have long life, ease and happiness at any price. This leads mankind into a feverish search for those three illusory targets, and the devil take the hindmost. In other words the Jack Principle is derived from Self Love, or negative charity[55].

## Self Determined and Other Determined

Searching for long life, comfort and happiness, man directs his attention outwards upon his environment, and expresses himself by modifying it, for instance into elaborate buildings, clothes and ornaments, or into a health service. He sees these modifications as means to achieve his aims, but eventually they become aims themselves and he finds himself dependent upon these manufactured externals for the apparent fulfilment of his original desires, long life, comfort and happiness.

His life therefore becomes determined not by a balanced response to himself and the notself, his environment, the other; but excessively determined by that other, the environment, upon which he has become so dependent. Hence the derivation of the pair of opposites, "self determined" and "other determined". Man through the action of the Jack Principle is excessively other determined[134].


## Displacement Activities

Because he is excessively other determined and pursues the delusory aims of long life, comfort and happiness through his dependence on the environment, man develops many activities in order to satisfy his inner need, driven to this by the Jack Principle. These illusory, displacement actitivies, are so called because they are alternatives to what his real aim should be.

Man's activities are almost all of the displacement type. He would do anything — or almost anything — rather than face his neglected internal states, so he chunters away gambling or hoarding money; celibate or promiscuous; judge or criminal; striving after health until he makes himself sick, because he is so frightened of dying or having a pain. He really is in a mess.

Yet he does not want to know he is in a mess. He would rather paper over the cracks in his personality with pills or alcohol, which blot out the anguish for a few hours, than face his internal disorder. So he staggers along dominated by the dreadful Jack Principle — other determined — and living by displacement activities.

It is no wonder that he has the sort of Health Care he has. It is the product of his own demands. Illness starts with the giving up situation. There is a serious, or apparently serious, set back to some displacement activity. It seems as if his whole being is threatened. Completely identified with this, our Jack suffers from a loss of the feeling that he is responsible for himself as a unique individual. He gets a sharp attack of the Job feeling. Everything seems to have turned against him, even his god the Jack Principle. He gives up. He gets sick [48],[45].

Then he takes himself to his doctor because he feels he needs fixing. His doctor is a fixer whose own ego is inflated by patching up deflated egos. That is his displacement activity, so Jack gets his pills. If he gets better everyone is satisfied. If he doesn't — his doctor becomes sick too because he is a failure.

This may sound an hilarious situation. It isn't. It is part of the reality behind the glossy intellectual facade, and the piles of equipment. Of course it is not only like that for the 'health and disease', 'doctor and patient', pairs of opposites. It is the same for every pair of relationships in the whole of our civilisation.


### I am not my body

Most people believe themselves to be their bodies. So as long as the body is not troubling them, and they are comfortable and not feeling frustrated or unhappy, they think they are alright. Therefore they tend not to ask for help until the body is not functioning well. By this time the disease may be far advanced and relatively little can be done by ordinary medical treatment (Allopathy). This leads to practitioners of all therapies being swamped by advanced disease. They have so little time to spend on preventive medicine. Most doctors feel frustrated by this.

The second consequence of the feeling of 'I am my body' is a refusal to recognise the importance of taking responsibility for one's mental state. A common reaction to being offered a choice of psychological treatment which might cure him, or a life on pills which will suppress his symptoms at the cost of some side effects and never cure him, is for the patient to say "Gimme the pills, Doc".

This failure to take responsibility for one's "Inner World"[230] leads to experiencing life only in the not self — the outer world and so is another reason why people are, in general, other determined.

### The Scientists' Retreat from Feeling into Technology

Feeling 'I am my body', and being other determined makes one excessively interested in the physical world, because it seems from these view points to be the only reality. So people are both materialistic and physically orientated and this conditions their thought and science. Most people who become scientists, certainly almost all in their youth, have abandoned their inner world of feeling and retreated into a materialistic technological attitude towards everything, including their fellow men.

Medical training is particularly prone to do this. The situations encountered are heart rendingly distressing and often disgusting, yet they have to be dealt with, so a retreat from feeling is inevitable, and displacement activities are developed. One of the easiest is to become a brittle and unemotional technocrat, a specialist. A few become callous. Some, when the pressures from their suppressed emotions have had time to build up, break down or kill themselves. Doctors have a higher than average suicide rate.

## The Psychological Defences of Technology

If one has constructed a theory, the easiest way of defending it is to state that any other theory which is not consistent with it is wrong, and can therefore be ignored. This is *The Ostrich's Head Defence*, to any awkward new idea. It is derived from the rather charming habit ostriches have of burying their heads in the desert sands when they feel too hard pressed, and there is no cover. A common example of this defence is to say, without making the slightest effort to understand the offending hypothesis, "It's not Scientific".

When circumstances are not suitable for ignoring the awkward fact or hypothesis, the next defence is to undermine its premises by suggesting the observation was not accurate, or the conditions of the experiment were not properly controlled, or statistically in error. Anything to give it immediate discredit so that its awkward potentialities do not have to be considered. This is the *Defence by Instant Defamation*.

If the intruder is too persistent, a belittling explanation, the *It's only so and so Defence*, comes into operation. The new idea is rationalised in terms of the already known. In this way the defender's system is preserved intact again and the possibly startling potential of the new idea is comfortably explained away.

While these defences are being progressively unfolded — laughter, ridicule, anger and rejection may be used against the purveyor of the supposedly offending and disturbing new idea. This is the *Defence by Negative Emotion*.

When these defences do not daunt the disturber of displacement activities the next move is to the *Doomed Trial Defence*. A test of the new idea is arranged, but in such unpropitious conditions that the apparatus or demonstrator cannot operate effectively, or the key observers may unavoidably be called away, so the trial is the flop it was meant to be.

Until now the defences described are almost all unconscious mechanisms. The defenders feel that it is perfectly right for them to behave as they do, and even feel magnanimous about offering their impossible trial, but there are a few hardened sceptics who manipulate these defences with deliberate intent. However the last defence is always operated consciously. The subconscious emotional disturbances having risen to the surface of the mind and transformed thinking and feeling to such an extent that action in the form of deliberate behaviour becomes impossible to avoid. There may be some restraining shreds of conscience remaining, but they get brushed aside. This ultimate defence is called *The Best Defence*. The title is taken from the saying "The Best Form of Defence is Attack".

*The Best Defence* takes many forms, loss of grants for the proposed research, loss of job, loss of a career, even imprisonment. Remember Dr. Frederick Axham who was attacked by being struck off the medical register and never reinstated. His 'infamous' conduct was that of supporting Sir Herbert Barker the great manipulator[96]. Remember Ruth Drown and Wilhelm Reich, both of whom died in penitentiaries in the U.S.A. in old age. The first because she held that radiesthesia worked, and the second because he sold healing instruments using the power of Orgone. Execution is seldom employed today. However, this need not take place openly as in the Middle Ages when torture would certainly have been added in. Today *The Best Defence* may even take the form of sorcery; see World Medicine's attack on Ivan Illich, where the front cover showed his wax effigy burning[235].

It takes a lot of callous prejudice to arrive at this level of absurdity or tragedy. A mature person should always, when faced with inflexible and hostile opposition be prepared to play the apostate. He can then survive to come again another day, or let time erode the defences. Rigidity cannot be sustained for ever; it leads to its own decay.

Le Shan has given a more scholarly account of the non-acceptance of the paranormal and reviewed the work of several others who have written in this field. Their main conclusion is that people are frightened by anything which upsets their "model of the universe" and defend it strongly[125].

> "I am not out to attack scientific research or scientific medicine in any sense. My aim is to show that in this scientific medicine there is a mine of opportunity for a much wider knowledge than can be allowed by modern methods, and above all by the current outlook on the world. We have no wish to scoff at the scientific mode of observation, but on the contrary to give it a true foundation. When it is founded on the spirit then, and only then, does it assume its full significance."
>
> Rudolf Steiner 26 October, 1922[180]

This reasonable approach is followed in this book. Two more quotations, this time from Dr. Franz Hartmann are as relevant today as in 1898.

"Science comes from man; wisdom belongs to God. Of sciences there are many; wisdom is only one. The sciences should be cultivated, but wisdom not be neglected, for without wisdom no science can exist"[81].

"An explorer must be a scientist, but not every scientist is an explorer. The majority of our modern schools of medicine produce nothing new, but merely deal in goods in whose production they had no share"[82].

## CHAPTER 2

# Acupuncture

Acupuncture is widely used in the Far East, mainly in Japan, China, Korea, Malaysia and Tibet. It should be regarded as only a physical part of the much greater whole, Oriental Therapy (chapter 11), but it is given a full exposition because it is well known in the West. It first took root in France having been brought back there by Jesuit Missionaries, but it is spreading fast.

### Theory

The body is conceived as a condensation of atoms around the centre of a number of vibrating, inter-reacting spirals of energies which form a force field that holds the physical body in existence. These spirals are organised into three main systems controlling:—

a) The Nerves,
b) The Digestion, of air and food,
c) The Circulation, including sex.

These divisions correspond to Ectoderm (skin and nervous system), Endoderm (organs of digestion) and Mesoderm (muscles, skeleton and blood vessels). The organs of the body are controlled by minor spirals which are part of the organisation just mentioned. The similarity of these divisions to those made by Rudolf Steiner (chapter 4) should be noted.

Where the energy spirals cut the surface of the body are active points, sited in indentations on the surface of the skin about a centimetre in diameter. When a finger is lightly rubbed over one of these points a slight scratchy, or sticky sensation is felt by the examiner. Certain of them are painful to pressure when the organ or system they are related to is disturbed; others have a regulating action.

The lines on the surface of the body which join these points are called meridians and are named after the organ or function with which they correspond. They bear no relation to the allopathic anatomical sites of the organs of the body, but do have a developmental basis for their situations. Along these lines an energy called Ki or Ch'i ebbs and flows with a diurnal rhythm, like the tides. Disturbances in the flow of this life force (Ki) affect the organs and systems of the body and mind, and produce diseases. The presence of organs in the skin under-lying acupuncture points has been described by Prof. Kim Bong Han of Korea[119], but the so called Bonghan corpuscles have not been confirmed by the Chinese[89].


Diagnosis

The meridians are used in diagnosis. On them lie the points which are tender to light pressure in disease and indicate which organs are disordered. History and pulse palpation of considerable complexity are also used to find out what is wrong. In Britain many publications and charts relate a single symptom to several possible acupuncture points. The use of these lists or charts alone to treat symptoms seems rather casual considering that every individual is unique, but they may be useful for quick first aid treatment.

Diagnosis can also be made with a pendulum over a radial diagram using the radiesthetic faculty (see chapter 13), and by sensing the patient's illness, which produces pain on the body of the diagnostician at points corresponding to where the patient being examined needs the insertion of needles. However, this method is only used by a few "sensitives" who have this faculty.

Recently Dr. Hiroshi Motoyama of Tokyo has developed an electronic apparatus for measuring the function of the meridians and their corresponding organs, using a computor to analyse the pattern of decay of an impulse of electrical current delivered at points on the tips of the fingers where the meridians end (seiketsu points)[139][140].

## Treatment

Treatment is mostly by the insertion of needles of various types, according to whether stimulation or sedation of the affected organ or system is required, and by heating or vibrating the needle. Pressure can be used instead of needles. A piece of the plant Artemesia can be allowed to smoulder directly on the skin. This is called Moxa. An alternative to Moxa is to use a pre-heated hammer.

When the needle is correctly inserted into an acupuncture point a peculiar deep painful sensation is experienced which spreads around the point of insertion. This is the view of two experienced Chinese trained European acupuncturists, but the Chinese Master Wu Wei P'ing states that needle insertion is painless[236]. Many needles may have to be inserted to cure a disorder. Skilled practitioners state that repeated pulse examinations, the time of day, season of the year, age, sex, as well as the radiesthetic and psychic phenomena previously mentioned, should control the treatment. After recovery there may have to be a re-balancing of the patient's forces by further needle insertions. The possibility that this rebalancing may be necessary should always be considered.

## Governing Body

The Acupuncture Association and Register Ltd., 34 Alderney Street, Westminster, London SW1, is the governing body in England. There are 9 regional offices. Anyone can practice Acupuncture in this country. The Acupuncture Association publishes a year book and register of the qualified acupuncturists, and encourages the public to consult them in choosing a suitably qualified practitioner. It is concerned to have official registration for all practising acupuncturists. There are about 125 registered acupuncturists in this country, and over 1,000 in practice in France[43].

## Comments

The author has no personal experience of treatment by acupuncture, but knows several patients who have had benefit from it and several who have not. He is favourably impressed by the use of finger pressure (Shiatsu)[41][42] as a first aid measure on himself, wife and friends. He travels with a pocket manual of Shiatsu[121].

Those who experience the treatment feel the odd deep pain on the initial insertion of the needles which soon disappears. Their disease when successfully treated disappears rapidly in a few seconds for a cramp, in a few minutes for a sting or in a few hours for something like cystitis. Arthritis goes away gradually.

There is only one minor criticism. There have been cases of infective hepatitis (jaundice) reported as being transmitted by acupuncture needles from one patient to another. Since this disease has a very long incubation period, the connection between the needles and jaundice probably escaped the originators of the system, and it seems clear that the time honoured method of keeping the needles clean is not adequate. One of the best innovations to arise from the National Health Service has been the disposable syringes, needles and lancets — use once and throw away. Sterilisation, unless of the highest quality is uncertain and expensive.

There are many books on Acupuncture, and it is difficult to choose a few to give as references. For the author, *Acupuncture and the Philosophy of the Far East* by George Ohsawa[144] and *Chinese Acupuncture* by Wu Wei P'ing are the most meaningful[226]. *The Acupuncture Handbook* by D. & J. Lawson-Wood[119] is practical, brief and links acupuncture with Homoeopathy (chapter 8). *The Yellow Emperor's Classic of Internal Medicine* translated by Ilza Veith, University of California Press, is famous but like all translations of ancient books, is difficult to relate to the present scene[210].

## CHAPTER 3

# Allopathy

An earnest student once asked his tutor "What is mind?". "No matter," said the Don anxious to get away. "What is matter?", persisted the student, "Never mind," said the Don with finality, making his escape. Probably the best formulation of the reaction between mind and body is given in the Mahabharata which is nearer five than three thousand years old.

> There are two classes of disease — bodily and mental. Each arises from the other. Neither is perceived to exist without the other. Of a truth mental disorders arise from physical ones, and likewise physical disorders arise from mental ones.
> Mahabharata: Santi Parva, XVI 8-9 [202]

Hippocrates first coined the term Allopathy. It comes from the Greek word "allos" meaning "other", and "pathee" meaning "anything that befalls one, hence suffering". The idea expressed by Hippocrates was that some diseases were produced by influences other than human, such as climate, radiation, magnetic and planetary influences. The other sort of diseases he called Homoeopathic, "homos" meaning "same", because they arose from disturbances within the person which to him included mind and body.

## Theory

As the tendency towards materialism began to increase the original meanings were changed. The homoeopathic was lost sight of, to be revived in a somewhat different form by Hahnemann as Homoeopathy (chapter 8), and in modern times as Psychotherapy (chapter 12). The Allopathic outlook was assumed to be the whole story. Gradually a vast body of information was built up on how the body breaks down. During the past century as technical and scientific methods rapidly developed, this has expanded enormously. In this system of therapy chemical compounds and surgery are used to interfere with the processes of breakdown which are called diseases. They operate mainly by competing for sites where chemical reactions take place, or by denaturing the enzymes which bring about the chemical reactions.

Sometimes efforts are made to prevent diseases happening as in immunisation and the reduction of animal carriers of invasive organisms; and if this is not possible, to stop the disease process by blocking it at source, as in replacement treatment for some anaemias, gland and vitamin deficiencies; or in the case of infection by eliminating the infecting organisms with antiobiotics.

In neoplastic disorders (growths in the widest sense) surgery, radiation and selective poisoning of the malignant tissues with drugs called antimitotics give a good measure of success. In other diseases, if the process is not self limiting or destructible, it is interfered with by introducing drugs, either to slow up or block its progress, such as the antimitotics already mentioned, or insulin in diabetes. If this cannot be done, drugs are used to alleviate the pain or other symptoms. Thus tranquillisers are given for anxiety, anti-depressants for depression and so on.

It is the chronic type of disease mentioned in the preceding paragraph that allopathy treats worst, and in which most toxic effects of the drugs used occur. Nevertheless at all times vigorous efforts are made to ensure that no drug is used unless it has been proven to do what it is intended to do; that its toxic effects are known, predictable and are at an acceptably low level.

However, it has to be said that mistakes occur and it is best to wait three to five years before using a new drug, unless it has outstanding advantages.

## Diagnosis

An effort is made to fit the history of the illness, the patient's appearance, and bodily abnormalities to a classification of diseases arrived at by a detailed physical study of the structure and chemical changes of the body in life and after death. The examination is detailed and rigorous. There are hundreds of biochemical, blood, breathing and electrical tests. X-rays are used to outline organs, and recently the whole body can be scanned in a few minutes using radio isotopes and a computor. The insides of hollow organs can be examined using flexible telescopes, and specimens of tissue removed for examination.

Again it has to be said that some investigations are so invasive, that they carry a small morbidity and may even cause a few deaths. But such are not undertaken unless the risks of not doing them would be greater. However, when a new investigative technique such as cardiac catheterisation is being explored, safety may not always be the first consideration.

## Treatment

Pills, injections and surgical operations are the fashion today. Liquid medicines are less used than they used to be, as they keep less well, are bulkier to store and more costly to prepare.

## Governing Body

The General Medical Council, 44 Hallam Street, London, keeps a register of medical practitioners and supervises the qualifying examinations, the professional conduct of doctors and their relationships with other methods of healing.

There are about 35,000 General Practitioners, about 12,500 Hospital Consultants and about 17,000 Junior Hospital Doctors. Four organisations, equivalent to Trades Unions, represent the doctors' interests.

The British Medical Association, BMA House, Tavistock Square, London WC1, has 50,300 members in the U.K., mostly General Practitioners.

The Hospitals Consultants and Specialists Association, Old Court House, London Road, Ascot, Berks., has 5,000 members, all hospital doctors, and no general practitioners. Some remain members of the BMA.

The Junior Hospital Doctors Association, 199B Temple Chambers, Temple Avenue, London EC4, has 4,600 members some of whom also belong to the BMA. The HCSA and the JHDA are about to unite to form a Federation of Hospital Doctors.

The Medical Practitioners Union, 10-26 Jamestown Road, London NW1, is a section of the Association of Scientific, Technical and Managerial Staffs and caters for both General Practitioners and hospital doctors. It will not give figures of separate sections of the ASTMS, but only a small minority of doctors are members.

## Comments

The Allopathic system is good for restoring acute biochemical and physical breakdowns and infections. It does less well when it tries to cope with chronic disorders, because it assumes disease is only physical and it interferes with the process after it is well established by artificial means which themselves carry a penalty. It is a very expensive and inappropriate way of dealing with social breakdown.

CHAPTER 4

# Anthroposophical Therapy

Rudolf Steiner, 1861–1925, preferred to call himself a spiritual scientist, rather than a mystic, but though he would have been called a mystic by many, his choice is correct. He had a scientific education at the Vienna Technical School, studying mathematics, natural history and chemistry, but also attended lectures on philosophy at the University, supporting himself by teaching[181][118]. Later he became a doctor of philosophy of Rostock University. All his life he maintained a rigorous experimental attitude to the information he obtained through his ability to be consciously aware of the super-sensible world at all levels including the spiritual. He was a rare being, a modern Jacob Boehme, with a scientific approach to his observations. To him everything was full of meaning and inter-related — the all was one.

His life work was in spiritual development. He founded the Anthroposophical Society, and lectured and taught extensively on how to attain spiritual vision. He painted, carved and used his faculty of spiritual vision to develop a theory and practice of colours. His ideas about medicine and agriculture developed out of replies to questions from people active in these fields. The "theory" was therefore the outcome of a specific encounter; he did not set out to create a body of super-sensual medical knowledge. This may be why his lectures do not lend themselves readily to systematic analysis.

## Theory and Practice

Steiner said "One . . . looks into the spiritual world, arrives at a conception of man . . . in health and disease, and then it is possible to found a kind of spiritualised medicine. . . . There can be no question of writing off empirical science as worthless and taking refuge in spiritualised science brought down from the clouds. That is quite the wrong attitude to adopt." "To knowledge of the physical man which is alone accessible to the Natural Scientific methods of today, Anthroposophy adds that of spiritual man"[182].

"All the results of the accepted Science of our time are derived in the last resort from the impressions of the human senses. For to whatever degree, in experiment or in observation with the help of instruments, man may expand the sphere of what is yielded by his senses, nothing in essence new is added by these means to his experience of the world in which his senses place him"[183].

Steiner's vision confirmed the Theosophical[22], and Indian Yogic view[234] that the physical bodies of all life forms are held in existence through the activity of a field of force working into the physical from the outside. He thought that everything must be brought into relation with the Universe and that in orthodox science today the processes that work in from the universe are ignored. "It is (thought) antiquated to relate human organs to the cosmos". He said that simple explanations are harmful, for "in all her manifestations, small or great, nature is highly complicated, never simple"[184].

He pointed out that the fields of force acting upon physical man are, starting from nearest the physical body and working outwards, the Etheric maintaining the physical body, instinctive consciousness and intuition; the Astral governing the field of the emotions, dreams and visions; the Mental, where ego activity and thought processes occur; and the Spiritual, the field of the soul.

Disharmonies in energy flow between these "higher bodies" of man produce disturbances in body and mind. The influences that do this arise from within the man himself and from outside him — from his environment, from the earth, from planetary influences of the Sun, Moon, Mercury, Venus, Mars, Jupiter and Saturn. Neptune and Uranus did not arise from this solar system, but were later attachments. Certain metals, gold, silver, mercury, copper, iron, tin and lead are related respectively to the first seven stars mentioned. They can be used therapeutically to correct disharmonies in the interrelationships of the higher bodies of man, which arise out of the processes affected by the seven stars influences.

There is also a correspondence between the stars and the anatomical organs and systems of the body. The Sun influences the heart, Mercury the lungs, Venus the kidneys, Mars the biliary system, Jupiter the liver and Saturn the nervous system.

Plants not only concentrate certain minerals, but certain parts of them are connected with various forces playing into them and man from the cosmos, and this should also be taken into account in using them medically. This view is similar to that held by Paracelsus, which is mentioned in the chapters on Herbalism (chapter 7) and Homoeopathy (chapter 8).

Steiner also accepted the principles of Homoeopathy, regarding it as a way of releasing the powers of substances developed in nature through the operation of forces coming from outside the earth, that is planetary and other cosmic influences. In Anthroposophical therapy, some of the therapeutic agents are used in a herbalist way — some homoeopathically [185].

Steiner made the point that in reality there are no allopaths because "what is described as an allopathic remedy is subjected within the organism to a homoeopathic process, and heals only through and by virtue of this process". He was here, I think, talking about herbal or chemical remedies administered in large doses, for he also said "the organism has no curative inter-reaction with the substances of the herbal world in their usual state. When they are taken into the body they are 'foreign' bodies causing really awful disturbances and over loading, if the body is burdened with the forces contained in allopathic doses"[186]. He must have been seeing into the future of side effects and iatrogenic diseases, when he said the methods in question often bring startling results in individual cases, and arouse illusory hopes, completely masking the danger in the background.

As regards diet Steiner said that meat eating leaves the job of digesting and developing vegetable food to the vegetarian animal eaten. So the meat eater does not maintain the power to do this as a vegetarian does. Therefore he does not develop the particular energies which he could produce from plant food. His plant food intake is wasted and he has to contend with energies peculiar to the animals he eats. The energies for overcoming plant food are there, but if not used they recoil into the organism with the effect of producing exhaustion and irritation. He says there is a considerable relief from fatigue if a vegetarian diet is adopted[187] [188]. I agree with him from personal experience. This is also the view held by practitioners of oriental medicine (chapter 11). Nevertheless Steiner was not a total vegetarian, nor is the author.

Steiner saw man as a being having three interweaving dynamic parts, the thinking, the feeling, and the instinct moving systems. The latter is known as the will in Steiner's nomenclature. It has a will of its own, but the most descriptive words are instinct and moving as will be seen in a moment.

The first of the parts is sited in the brain, nerves and sense organs. Its function is consciousness, control, thinking and form maintenance.

The second part of man is centered in the chest and consists of the lungs, heart blood and vessels. It is dynamic and rhythmic and spreads our awareness through the entire body. It takes in energies and excretes them. It carries out the functions of life, feeling and sense of self. It holds a balance between the first and third systems, whose interests often conflict.

The third organisation is the instinct moving system concerned with metabolism, reproduction and moving. It is centred in the abdomen, dealing with the conversion of food to bodily substance and subsequent energy exchanges and transformations. One is not aware of this aspect of its functioning but more aware of the workings of the muscular system. It is full of vitality and regeneration. It pays to be on good terms with one's instinct moving system. It certainly has a will of its own. Much psychosomatic disorder occurs when the nervous system and the instinct moving systems are at loggerheads, for unless they are in accord, the mental system's projects will not come to fruition, because there will not be enough energy, or there will be some physical symptom which has a distracting effect, or there will even be a disease. The effect of these reactions is a lack of ability to do. Hence the individual has no will.

Plants have the same three-fold structure, only upside down. The root, like the brain, is relatively inactive metabolically, isolated from external influences, yet controlling the situation. The stem and leaf systems in their intermediary position between root and flower, actively control the ebb and flow of water and salts, and correspond to the rhythmic system in man. The flower and fruit are metabolically active and mediate between the plant and the cosmos, as well as being responsible for reproduction, so they correspond to the instinct and moving systems of man.

These considerations lead to the choice of the right remedy for an illness — for a head disturbance such as a headache a root would be prescribed, for a heart remedy digitalis leaf is widely used, not only by the spiritual science but also in the allopathic and herbalist systems.

Steiner said that raw food influences man, and produces changes in him which he cannot by his own power avoid. By the subduing influences of fire, the raw material is changed so that the food becomes nutritive only. Cooking allows man to assert himself over food. If he did not cook, his eating would be a perpetual process of remedial treatment. This idea is echoed by the oriental therapeutic approach outlined in chapter 11, which does not recommend raw food except medicinally[189].

In addition to the methods above, heat and cold, skin stimulation by external plasters, massage, colour, and eurhythmic movements are used as forms of therapy directed at the harmonising of the relationships of the individual to the cosmos, the stars, of the individual and his four bodies, as well as the relationships between the three systems based on the anatomy of the physical body. Furthermore, all of these aspects of man influence each other[190].

The diagnosis of what is wrong with a sick person may be clear to a person with spiritual vision such as Steiner, but it is difficult for an ordinary person to achieve. It requires an ability to hold many inter-relating processes simultaneously in consciousness. The problem is not made easier because a physical symptom or sign may seem to be unrelated to the ordinary anatomy and physiology learnt by an allopathically trained doctor.

In diagnosis all the usual methods of allopathic medicine — a history, physical examinations and tests are used, as well as such spiritual vision as the practitioner has attained from practice of the meditation exercises described by Dr. Steiner, knowledge of his books on therapy and special training.

**Governing Body**

Information on Steiner's Spiritual Science may be obtained from the Anthroposophical Society, Rudolf Steiner House, 23 Park Road, London NW1. The Secretary of the Anthroposophical Medical Society has offices at 35 Park Road London NW1. This Society holds 5 day conferences bi-annually as well as other meetings.

There is no specific governing body of Anthroposophical medicine in this country. Prior Allopathic (medical) qualifications are required before commencing the study of the Steiner methods, which are taught at the Lucas Clinic, in Arlesheim, Switzerland, where long courses are held regularly. Shorter courses are also held regularly at the Goetheanum in Dornach, Switzerland as part of the activity of the Medical Section of the High School for Spiritual Science.

The insistence of a prior qualification keeps the numbers of practitioners down for reasons discussed under Homoeopathy in chapter 8. There are about 24 Anthroposophical medical practitioners in this country. In Germany and Holland there are nearly 1000, and many hospitals and clinics as well as a research centre[50].

The Weleda Company in Switzerland was founded 54 years ago to supply remedies and toilet preparations prepared to high standards from natural ingredients according to Steiner's principles. It has a branch or agency in many countries including Great Britain.

## Comment

Two patients I know avoided operations, one for acute appendicitis, the other for gall bladder disease, which would have been unavoidable under allopathic treatment, by use of Anthroposophical Therapy. In a slight personal experience of this form of therapy, I find Steiner products effective.

What Steiner said is not so far off the eastern idea of the anatomy of man described elsewhere, and discussed in chapter 11 on oriental medicine and in chapter 15 on the strategic solution. Nor is there a conflict between his ideas and those of Gurdjieff[73]. Anthroposophical Therapy is relatively ignored except in continental Europe today, but it is an all embracing way of life, integrating man with the cosmos, and this is also found in oriental medicine. T'ai Chi and Yoga are similar health giving ways of life but of course do not have special therapeutic divisions. All the other systems mentioned in this book, except Oriental Therapies, Chapter 11, are only methods developed from a limited view of man, or deal with only a part of man.

CHAPTER 5

# Body Dynamics

Chiropractic and Osteopathy, Alexander Technique,
Rolfing, Hatha Yoga, T'ai Chi, Comments.

The Allopathic System tends to dismiss displacements of the spine lightly as having little significant influence on human disease and prescribes analgesics for the pain. If the pain is severe and disabling, immobilisation by bed rest, traction, plaster casts and corsets is used. If these fail the operation of spinal fusion is performed. These treatments are not only costly and time consuming, but produce their own disabilities. Allopathic practitioners who manipulate are rare. Manipulation is taught at only one medical school in England, and there is the whimsically named BAMM (British Association of Medical Manipulators) which runs courses for medical practitioners on osteopathic lines. On the other hand the spine is taken seriously by the systems about to be discussed as well as by Radiesthetists, practitioners of Oriental Therapy and Healers who find that there is a close relationship between its disturbance and diseases.

## CHIROPRACTIC AND OSTEOPATHY

There is not a big enough difference between these two systems to justify dealing with them separately. Manipulation of the spine using similar methods is part of oriental therapy and therefore ancient. Techniques for splinting fractures are given in the Hearst Papyrus from Egypt of about 1500 B.C.[122]. Bonesetters have existed in Europe certainly from the Middle Ages.

In the United States of America, Osteopaths now do the same training as allopathic medical students with special training in manipulation and qualify with the M.D. (Doctor of Medicine) degree. Chiropractors have their own training schools and qualify with the D.C. (Doctor of Chiropractic) degree. They still assert their independence of the allopathic system. Both are legally recognised major systems in the U.S.A. with over 25,000 practitioners. In Europe the osteopaths and chiropractors have their own training schools and there is no official recognition.

Osteopathy was founded by Dr Andrew Still in the 1850's in the U.S.A. In 1895 Daniel Palmer, a healer, cured his caretaker of deafness by manipulation of his thoracic spine and started chiropractic. Still was convinced that disturbances of blood flow caused disease — hence "The rule of the Artery". Palmer favoured pressure on nerves — hence "The rule of the Nerve". Both were united in attributing to displacements, often minor, of the bones of the spine, the prior cause of the lesion however mediated.

### Theory

Displacements of joints are in themselves directly painful and disabling, or they may produce pain away from the main site of the dislocation in the same segment of the body — called referred pain. Each segment of the body has all its nerve supply from the corresponding level of the spinal cord.

In Oriental Therapy it is pointed out that the whole body is represented in every organ. So that correction of the disturbance in one organ results in a harmonisation of the whole person. This provides a basic principle of which osteopathy and chiropractic are special examples.

Displacements of the spine alter the shape of the openings through which the nerves mainly, but also the arteries, veins and lymphatics supplying the nerves, pass in and out from the spine to and from the organs. The resulting deformities in the openings disturb the function of the nerves, by pressing directly on them, or by altering the blood supply or lymphatic drainage. The information which the nerves take in from the organs, or pass out to them is altered and a disturbance of function or even disease occurs.

The functional disorders produced by such displacements will not cover the whole range of diseases humanity suffers from, but they will help some which are certainly difficult to treat by allopathic means. Examples of such conditions are asthma and allergies which often result from subluxations of the bones at the base of the neck (8th cervical to 3rd thoracic vertebrae). Headaches are another troublesome complaint often responding to manipulation of the relationships between the first and second cervical vertebrae and the skull.

It is not only methods of diagnosis of bone displacements, including clinical examination, x-rays and manipulation, that are taught in the well appointed schools of osteopathy (5 years) and chiropractic (4 years). Physiology, anatomy, pathology and pharmacology have a significant place in the syllabus. From the experimental divisions of these departments come interesting ideas on forms of treatment which could have applications in the allopathic system.

For example there is the neurocalometer which detects the level of a lesion in the spine, by detecting the slight change in temperature of the skin which occurs at the same level as the lesion due to interferences of the function of nerves supplying the blood vessels in the skin.

There is now a trend to look on the spine as consisting of a number of mobile vertebral functional units, and evaluate it in terms of movements that can and cannot be performed by the patient. This gives earlier diagnosis when the x-rays may still be normal.

## Diagnosis

The history of the disorder is important and is usually exhaustive. In addition, clinical examination of the spine and joints, x-rays, blood tests and the use of specialised instruments, such as the neurocalometer are the main methods of diagnosis.

## Treatment

Treatment is by manipulation. Usually where there is muscle tension and ligament tenderness associated with the displacement, massage and heat treatment precede the manipulation and render it easy and painless.

Osteopathy tends to use leverage more than chiropractic where the application of light sudden low amplitude force, while the patient is relaxed and suitably placed, springs the joint apart and directs it to move back into a correct position. In fact practitioners of both disciplines use either method. Chiropractors are not allowed by their Governing Body to use medicines of allopathic type, but they may use vitamins, minerals and glandular supplements. Diet and all the usual physiotherapy techniques are used.

## Governing Bodies

British Chiropractors' Association, 257 Woolton Road, Liverpool 16. 61 members. However there are many Canadian and American Chiropractors in practice in this country who may not be members.

The Anglo-European College of Chiropractic, Cavendish Road, Bournemouth, Hants, trains Chiropractors.

British Osteopathic Association, 16 Buckingham Gate, London SW1. 279 members. They publish the Osteopathic 'Blue Book' and a Directory of Members.

The Ecole Européenne d'Osteopathie, 28/30 Tonbridge Road, Maidstone, Kent, trains Osteopaths.

## Comments

A chance meeting at a conference with a Canadian Chiropractor gave a relieving personal experience of chiropractic manipulation to the author. He knows of several patients whose joints, backaches, asthma, nasal allergies, headaches and migraine have been relieved by chiropractors when allopathic treatment had failed. He has no personal experience of osteopathy, but thinks it works just as well.

Osteopathy and chiropractic are not applicable to the whole range of diseases, but their techniques will always be needed, and they will have an enduring place in health care.

There is a good account of chiropractic in "New Light on Therapeutic Energies" by Mark L. Gallert[60].

# ALEXANDER TECHNIQUE

Frederick Matthias Alexander was born in 1869 in Tasmania[9]. He became a reciter of poetry and humourous pieces, but was plagued by losing his voice. He reasoned that he was using his body wrongly, and studied himself to find the reason by using mirrors. He found that he was pulling his head back and tightening his throat every time he began to recite. He observed other people and found that the head leads in every movement of the body. The area of primary control was in the relationship between the neck and the dorsal spine at the site where many people develop what is absurdly called the "Dowager's Hump".

The trouble was this strange habit felt natural to him. The more he tried to correct it, the more it went wrong. He found that in order to stop throwing his head back, he had to learn not to do so. He had to say "I refuse to recite when told to do so". "I can tell the head to relax and not perform the wrong movements." "Then when I intend to recite I will direct my head first to lead forward and up." He practiced, got his control right and kept his voice.

Years before its time he had discovered a principle of Behaviour Therapy, that of consciously using a blocking thought to inhibit a habit and then substituting a new habit.

Alexander elaborated the idea, *Use Affects Function,* to cover many movements, and showed that getting up and sitting down demonstrated the working of his principle best, for people moving wrongly almost always throw their heads back first when making these movements. He found he could teach others with similar sorts of difficulty to heal themselves. A consequence of correcting the defects of movement lead to a sense of liberation, an increase in health and all round efficiency as a human being. If the training has been long enough to establish the new habits, the results are life long.

Considering that chiropractic and osteopathy and many healers stress the importance of maintaining the structural integrity of the spine, it is easy to see the importance of this relatively simple method and its use in prophylaxis.

## Governing Body

The Society of Teachers of the Alexander Technique, 3 Albert Court, Kensington Gore, London SW7. There are 170 teachers of the Alexander Principle in the world. Most are in and around London.

## ROLFING

Ida Rolf who works at Esalen, Big Sur, California U.S.A., developed this form of deep massage of the tissue planes. It is fairly painful as the knuckles are ground deep into the muscles to stretch the shortenings and adhesions of their fibrous sheaths which prevent a normal posture. The whole body is gone over at every session with special emphasis on a different aspect of the body at each one of the ten or more sessions. The posture, but not movement, is studied to plan the areas which require modification.

People who have been Rolfed, experience, as after learning the Alexander technique, an immense sense of well being. They walk tall. Some have an emotional catharsis during the experience – for a deep experience it is. Others have a character change for the better. Mostly the benefits obtained are lasting if the whole course is taken, but there is a tendency to relapse. There are probably only 3 or 4 trained Rolfers in this country. Enquiries can be made to Ida Rolf at Esalen, Big Sur, California, USA.

# HATHA YOGA

In England today many people practice Hatha Yoga which consists of postures, movements and breathing exercises, because it makes them feel good. They find they learn to live and work better, with an inner calm. They also become healthier.

Yoga is derived from the sanscrit word for union. The idea implies striving to attain the state of oneness, or unity with God. This certainly is not the aim of the average participant of the local yoga club, but it is surprising how some people change after they have been practising Hatha yoga. It seems to give rise to an inner development.

There are many more types of yoga than just the exercises and breathing. The two main Indian descriptions are found in the Bhagavad Gita and the Yoga Sutras of Patanjali. Numerous translations of these are available. There is a good summary of both in Ernest Wood's book on Yoga[234].

One of the results of practising Hatha yoga is the attainment of a sound spine. All those who are good at it, and practise regularly, are straight, upright and supple. The exercises seem to have an extraordinary loosening and correcting effect. They show up weaknesses however, and one frequently sees middle-aged enthusiasts giving themselves symptoms from bones pressing on nerve roots. Hatha yoga is alright if one is born into it, or young, but it is risky if older. There are other ways of spiritual development and health care.

This is no condemnation but a warning based on personal experience.

The breathing exercises and the postures also regulate the distribution of vital forces — the prephysical prana or Ki mentioned in Chapter 2 on Acupuncture, and in Chapter 11 on Oriental Therapy. These two actions — the correction of the spine and the control of prana are how Hatha Yoga improves the function of the body and mind.

## T'AI CHI

In Chinese T'ai Chi (pronounced Tie Jee) means Great Pole or Axis, and is usually translated as "Supreme Ultimate". The full title is T'ai Chi Ch'uan, the latter word meaning fist, and so boxing. But T'ai Chi is not really intended for fighting, this is a debasement of its initial use, which was a form of active meditation designed to relate the individual to the universe by concentrating the Ch'i (pronounced Chee), Japanese Ki, Prana in Sanscrit (see chapters 1 and 11), and regulate its flow. Ch'i is best thought of as a prephysical energy existing in the air.

T'ai Chi is said to have been invented by Taoist Monks who wished to occupy the restless activity of the children growing up in the monastery with something which, as they learnt it as a part of their play, would exert a profound and beneficial influence upon them. This is information given to me by a Chinese teacher of the art, who as a child learnt it as part of her education in Mainland China.

Once the basic sequence of movements has been learnt two people can use them in a contest of wits and skill, which has the advantage of rapidly showing up deficiencies in the basic movements and mental state of the players. From this developed its use as a means of self defence and fighting which has many variations.

The Solo exercise consists of 13 basic and 37 main postures with repetitions of 28 of these[34][38]. It is a slow relaxed ballet, like swimming in air, with breathing co-ordinated with the arm movements. The breath is taken in as the arms are extended outwards and upwards, and exhaled as the arms are contracted or brought down. The spine is straight, and its axis is always over the weight carrying foot. The waist is the other axis of the body. But the head, spine and heel of the weight carrying foot were always in line before the next movement began when the Chinese teacher, who allowed me to observe one of her classes was performing herself. This is in accord with the literal translation of T'ai Chi as Great Axis.

People who have done T'ai Chi all say that they are better for it, but as they were young and healthy they cannot give an account of its curative action. T.T. Liang, a Master of T'ai Chi, says he took it up to save his life after a serious illness, and at 75 years of age, had been practising it for 30 years[127]. Millions of Chinese feel the same, and can be seen practising the solo exercise morning and evening. Certainly T'ai Chi can be done at any age and is no strain, though it generates a surprising amount of heat. The essence of it is to be as relaxed and natural as a small child, to make no muscular effort or strain. This is a contrast to Hatha yoga where the exercises are much more demanding.

T'ai Chi is the most comprehensive of all the systems described in this chapter. It embraces everything — the relationship of mind and body, and of both to the universe. It is a way of life.

## Comments

In Chiropractic, Osteopathy, and Rolfing the practitioner plays the active part and manipulates the passive relaxed body of the patient, whose mind does not come into the process. In the Alexander method, Hatha Yoga and T'ai Chi the patient uses his mind to direct the relationship of the skull to the first two bones of the spine for this is the key to a varied range of symptoms. This is in accord with the Alexander

Method in which the leader of the movement is the back of the skull from which the head should feel suspended. The same is true for T'ai Chi for "When you can feel as if your head was suspended on a thread from above, your spirit of vitality will be raised, and the defects of obtuseness and clumsiness will be no more"[215]. From a slight personal experience of Hatha yoga, I think that a stoop was what seemed to worry the instructor most, not the inability of an ageing body to control itself. So the 'Great Axis' principle is common to the mentally active — self determinant group where the subject takes responsibility for himself. It is also present in the minds of some chiropractors, osteopaths and in the other systems of therapy mentioned in the introduction to this chapter.

To the author this ties up with the quotation from the Mahabharata mentioned at the beginning of the chapter on Allopathy which said that physical disorders arose from mental ones and vice versa, and with the idea of psychological 'centering' which is a common preliminary to many methods of meditation. The same idea underlies the title and message of John Lilly's book — *In the Centre of the Cyclone,*[128] and also relates to the seventeenth century Sir Thomas Browne, a Norwich doctor, who said in *Religo Medici* that there were "Allurements and baits of superstition to those vulgar heads that look asquint on the face of Truth, and those unstable judgments that cannot consist in the narrow point and centre of Virtue without a reel or stagger to the Circumference". The centre is still. Here is the real point of relationship to the circumference[26].

CHAPTER 6

# Healing

Healing through an inter-personal relationship, without the intervention of a physical agent, such as medicine, a tool, or a machine, has been known from pre-Christian times in many parts of the world. Hand Healing is used in Oriental Therapy which is about 3000 years old, and the Kahunas brought this ancient method of healing (Huna) to Polynesia about 2000 years ago[131][132][133].

**Theory**

Reading widely on the subject, discussing with at least 10 effective healers their own ideas on how they heal, and their methods of doing so, provides complete confirmation of the law which states that every human being is a unique individual. All healers work, or think they work in different ways. The following tentative exposition of healing is to help a newcomer to the field to understand the subject. It certainly is not final, or completely correct, for healing is at an important growing point at present. What really matters is not how something works, but that it does work — and healing does work.

The first thing to realise is that the healer does not do the healing — he acts as a guide for the transmission of healing.

This follows from the action of the principle that "Thought directs Energy". Secondly a request is almost invariably made to whoever or whatever controls the power to do all that is necessary to eliminate the problem, if that is the right thing to do.

There are two main divisions of healing, that using pre-physical energies such as Prana or Ki, and that using energies other than the pre-physical, the so called spirit or spiritual healing. According to the principle that "What one believes to be true, either is true or becomes true in one's mind, within limits to be determined experimentally or experientally", opinion may differ widely as to the explanation offered for the theory of healing, yet these two main divisions are accepted by most healers, or are inherent in their writings. However, probably owing to the principle just given, many would disagree with this explanation. This is because their beliefs differ. Such beliefs are limits which can and should be transcended[129].

The pre-physical energies need a physical basis to direct them, so most of this type of healing is done by use of the hand. If the healer is one of those people who naturally accumulates excess amounts of Prana or Ki, he does not need a preliminary storage of it, by breathing or exercises, as in the oriental system of healing. He places his hands on or near the patient, or the affected part of the patient, and mentally directs the force to pass into the patient and heal him. A few people can direct energy to pass to a patient at long range, but usually the distance must be relatively small, about arms length or some form of physical contact is used. Sometimes if the healing energy is great and the need also, no mental direction is required, and the contact may be slight, just the touch of a robe.

The other types of healing involve contact either with the world of disincarnate spirits, or the individual's higher self.

Possibly these are not mutually exclusive alternatives, and one healer will do it one way, another the other, and some both ways. Once contacted the spirits or the healer's higher-self are asked to heal the patient. This form of healing can be instantaneous and occur over long distances.

The experience of mediums, clairvoyants, and others such as Emanuel Swedenborg[218], shows there are many unpleasant and untrustworthy beings in the spirit world, but there are many of great understanding, who can, because they are discarnate, change the nature of a person more easily than by other methods. Clairvoyants, Spiritualists, and many others also state that each one of us has one or two spirits that guide and help us. The Huna, the Oriental and the Christian teaching is that each of us has a higher self, and that there is a world of higher selves. Possibly the modern spiritualist and the Huna ideas are not very far apart. None of this is at variance with ancient Egyptian and Oriental thinking, but it is not in accord with modern western thought, scientific philosophical and religious.

The healers who perform by the action of the disincarnate spirits are not conscious of their action. They make a request and may receive a mental answer as a voice heard, or just an idea; some use table rapping or an Ouija board, but the actual healing takes place invisibly to all of them.

Those healers who know they perform through the higher self may be quite unconscious of its action except that their patient changes. Some are aware of the process to varying degrees and take a conscious part in directing the reharmonisation of their patients, but know that they do not act from the personality. Others think they heal, because their personalities have rationalised the event in their own favour, operating as the personality always does on the Jack Principle (see chapter 1). They may not even have heard of the higher Self. This is another reason for healers varying so much in their explanations of their talent.

The disorder may be sensed through the hand passed like a slow scanner over the patient some way off the body — or it may be sensed by mental scanning of the body and the disturbance appreciated either in the hand of the healer, or his own body, or in his mind, or sensing may take place by visualisation of the disturbance of the patient's energy fields, or by sharing his emotional and mental disturbance. As the disturbances are sensed they are balanced and harmonised. Sometimes the healer will realise that this is neither possible nor desirable. He will then have to decide consciously to stop or go on. A wise healer follows his intuition on this.

Another way of healing can take place through out-of-the-body-experience. Either while asleep, or sometimes during the day when it is an exhausting experience, a healer's mind may pass from around his body to any distance and heal another ill person. He may be aware of this happening, or he may not. Such experiences are described by Dr Arthur Guirdham who has written extensively on the subject [72].

Sometimes healers perceive that special houses, and even whole localities, are harmful to a certain person. In other instances another person can be damaging, or the disease may arise from an object or a noise. Unless such relationships are changed the effects of any treatment will only be temporary. It goes almost without saying that personal adjustment in a way of life or total psychological change may likewise be needed, but they are often brought about by the healing itself.

The faith or belief of a sufferer and that of the healer have no strong influence on healing. Many previously sceptical healers have found that they could heal by accident — many of the cured have been sceptics. Healing is not "God given" any more than a table is "God given". Since thought directs energy, no one wishing another person well, or praying for him, will fail to help that person, but only a healer will cure him. Healers are rare. This is why so few in holy orders can heal by this method, though many practise the laying on of hands at healing services where prayer is the basis. This also applies to Christian Science practitioners — some of whom are healers.

It is clear that occasionally a belief held by the sufferer and prayer to God does induce healing. The evidence of this is in the less than 100 carefully documented cures that have resulted from the millions of invalids who have visited Lourdes. Healers in our own country have cured many thousands from fewer numbers of sufferers in a shorter space of time than Lourdes has been operating.

**Practice**

People who are being healed by the first, or close proximity method, may take some time to get better, if the condition is long standing. Stiff joints need time to loosen and nerves to recover. The patient may experience nothing at all, or notice tingles, or jerks and twitches, heat or cold. Others feel their nerves working while the healing is going on but they are not being touched. It felt "as if a small rat was moving in my back" one woman said. Several treatments are almost always needed.

Some have emotional disturbances, which may have induced the illness, released by healing. They can have a disturbing emotional catharsis. Of those people healed by the second method, some are instantaneously cured, but have to be loosened up if the disability has been long standing, others respond more slowly and need several sessions.

Harry Edwards states that Spiritual Healing fails to cure only

20% of those who attend him. This is a remarkable claim. If it was substantiated it indicates a better cure rate than other systems, since many of the patients he healed were considered to be incurables of many years standing. Yet no serious effort has been made, either by the Medical Profession, or the Church, to investigate his claim in a prospective study, in spite of his offers to co-operate in this[46].

Others healers estimate their failure rate at 30% but none of those interviewed estimated a failure rate of more than 60%. When one realises that practically all the cases that come to healers are people who all those of other persuasions cannot cure, and none of whom have self limiting diseases, these proportions are impressive.

## Psychic Surgery

Psychic Surgery does not only take place in the Philippines, though it is mainly in Manila that the conjurors are found. It is a phenomenon that occurs in Indonesia, Malaysia, Thailand and Tibet. The real thing goes on in poor back streets and villages illegally. I have talked to people who have been there, had it done and felt better for it, though none had any objective proof, except one possibly who had his eyes treated for a slight cataract and can now see clearly.

I have seen several films of it being done. In one the operator pointed his finger held about 6 inches off the skin covering a cyst, and made a short movement downwards. Instantaneously a cut appeared which bled, then he put his fingers in, worked the cyst loose and took it out. His hands were bare to the elbow. It is difficult to think how that example could be faked.

However, the film called the Psychic Surgery, Miracle or Illusion shown on ITV in April 1975 proves without doubt that some Philippino healers are, as far as the surgical side of their technique is concerned, just illusionists. None of the patients treated in that film improved. But even if this aspect of psychic surgery is only impressive make believe manufactured by sleight of hand, this does not mean that some may not be real hand healers.

In psychic surgery passes are made over the patient's body and the disorder worked down into the abdomen. The operator then starts to dig with fingers of both hands, with a movement best described as scrabbling. As he goes deeper, blood appears and is wiped away. His hands seem to enter the abdominal cavity. Eventually after much scrabbling a piece of tissue is removed. Sometimes it is human, sometimes animal, sometimes it is an object made of metal or paper. The blood when analysed is usually not human. Then the operator makes movements as if pulling the edges of the wound together, there is a final scrabbling and no wound!

People who have had it done say it feels slightly uncomfortable, that the surgeon's hands feel deep inside them, but it is not distressing. It looks very impressive.

True Believers think that the healer dematerialises the disease and then rematerialises it in a form which can be extracted through the patient's abdominal cavity by his manipulations. When asked why not just do straight hand healing because it is so much less effort in a hot and sweaty climate, they reply that there is an element of religious drama to the ceremony which appeals to the Philippinos' temperament. They like it that way.

At present Manila is the Lourdes of the Far East with enterprising package tour operators selling a visit to the Philippines with "Psychic Surgery" as its main attraction. However, serious minded observers consider that there is something in it and that some operators, like Tony Agpao, are real healers[219].

## Governing Body

During the last 30 years the public's attitude to healing has gradually warmed, in spite of discouraging official reports. By 1960 over 200 Hospital Management Committees in the N.H.S. had decided to allow spiritual healers to attend their patients in hospitals. These decisions were endorsed by their medical advisory committees of hospital doctors. The present situation, which was confirmed by the Department of Health and Social Security in 1974, is that Healers can visit patients in all hospitals of the N.H.S. provided they are members of the National Federation of Spiritual Healers and their services are requested by, and agreeable to the patient, or his representative, if he is unable to act on his own behalf.

The National Federation of Spiritual Healers, Short Acres, Church Hill, Loughton, Essex. Promotes the study and practice of healing. It has 5,000 members and 3,000 individual practising healer members. It is a registered charity, and runs study courses in healing, but does not have a qualifying examination.

The Churches Council of Healing, and the Churches Fellowship of Psychical and Spiritual Studies, St. Mary Abchurch, Abchurch Lane, London ECN 7BA, are other organisations which interest themselves in the subject, and have knowledge of those who heal. They have the impractical policy of trying to ensure that healing is done only in and through the Church. The world wide distribution, and pre-Christian existence of healers in all races and all religions makes this unrealistic. Here is an example of the tendency of organisations to make only decisions favourable to themselves mentioned in the first chapter.

There are many other local associations of healers, some at county level, others are small groups of individuals. Some of these are affiliated to the N.F.S.H. Many healers remain isolated individuals, for the ability to heal is a very personal thing.

It is difficult to estimate the numbers of those who heal in Britain today. Most who do are people who prefer peace and quiet, and have other occupations. They do not charge for their services. However, a fair estimate would be just over 20,000 healers. Considering that healers give their services free, do not advertise and are not a state monopoly, this may sound startling, for it puts healing in the same class as the National Health Service with its 50,000 doctors. Moreover healing is very acceptable to those at the top of the social ladder, and to the establishment who for years have been quietly having their difficult disorders healed.

**Comments**

Anyone with the right intention and knowledge can learn to manipulate Prana or Ki, and heal by the first, close proximity method. The ability to perform the second type of healing — spirit or spiritual, comes with growth as a real human being, it cannot be learnt, but many people who do not heal may find it possible to do so when shown how to go about it.

Healing is the only way to cure severe progressive disorders, other than by destructive methods such as surgery, radiation or cell poisons, when the process has gone beyond all the other methods of therapy. It does not require expensive equipment or large teams of people as does allopathic treatment.

It is potentially the most important of all methods of therapy. There is the probability that everyone could learn self-healing. The oriental method of self-healing called Do-in in Japan and Shiatsu in China, is practised by Zen Buddist monks, (see chapter 11), and can be learnt by anyone in a few lessons, once they have understood the philosophy[41][42]

This study of healing and healers was made before reading Lawrence Le Shan's research on the subject. I find nothing to disagree with in his findings and comments. He is to be congratulated on his thorough approach, but even more on his practical "Do-it-Yourself" attitude which led to his discovering he could heal, and to helping others find they had the same talent. His book should be read by everyone interested in the subject[126]. A brief but thoughtful article on healing has recently been published by Isaacs[99], and a book which contains a good deal of profound information on the subject is *Esoteric Healing* by Alice A. Bailey[6].

Healing has a big future. Luckily for the public the way is open for Healers to use their talents in the National Health Service. Let us not only think of the money that would be saved, but also of the advantages to the sick. Nevertheless the time will soon come when whole time healers will have to consider their attitude to remuneration.

CHAPTER 7

# Herbalism

It is probable that ever since early humans watched sick animals eating special plants and curing themselves, herbal treatment has been used. There are herbal remedies in the texts of Ayurvedic medicine of about 5000 BC, the Pen Tsao, or Great Herbal of China 3000 BC, ancient Assyria, Egypt, Greece and Rome, down to the present day.

Culpeper wrote the most famous English Herbal published in 1653. An important modern one is Otto Gessler's, *Die Gift und Arzneipflanzen von Mitteleuropa* published in 1953. Until the last 100 years the allopathic British Pharmacopaeia contained hardly anything except the old herbal remedies which made up about 80% of its content. This proportion has rapidly changed as the manufacture of organic chemicals developed, until in 1963 the BP contained only 6.5% drugs of plant origin[93].

## Theory

Many old herbalists thought herbs had astrological affinities with planets and zodiacal signs. Astrologers state that the sun signs are associated with different types of disease and tendencies for parts of the body to give trouble. Some stress the importance of picking the plants at astrologically suitable times. Culpeper and Paracelsus were two who thought in this way. This aspect has been ignored in recent times, but now that Gauquelin[63] has demonstrated that there is an association between the sun sign and life occupation it seems these ideas would be worth exploring anew, and this has been done in the Secret Life of Plants[207].

Putting aside astrological considerations there are three other ways in which herbs work. Firstly there is the direct chemical action, in the allopathic way of one or more active principles contained in the plant, which interferes with the sequence of chemical changes that are part of the disease process. A pharmacologically active principle may be an alkaloid such as reserpine, which seems to be the most influential one found in Rauwolfia Serpentina – the snake root.

In the whole plant several similar active principles are packaged in a biologically elaborated complex of proteins, enzymes, trace elements, inorganic salts, chlorophyll, vitamins, terpenoids, polycelluloses, glucosides and phenols. Such a complex has been found by experience to be easily assimilated and to produce far fewer undesirable side effects than concentrated "purified" active principles. Rauwolfia has been in use for thousands of years in Ayurveda as a sedative; Gandhi used to drink Rauwolfia tea as a night cap. Yet it has only taken 20 years for its most active alkaloid, reserpine, to start to go out of fashion because, although good for lowering blood pressure and sedation, it can cause severe depression and carcinoma of the breast.

The lack of toxicity of herbal remedies is due to their containing many active principles which act in different ways reinforcing each other's effects. This is called Synergism. When investigated singly the constituents of a herbal remedy may appear inert yet when taken together their synergistic action has a pharmacologically measurable effect. Further the other substances in the whole plant modify the harsh action of a single active principle.

Thirdly, plants grow according to a pattern and some of their healing properties are derived from this. The idea that things have a signature or pattern is old. The ancient Egyptians had it, and Jacob Boehme, the German Mystic, wrote about it in a work called *The Signature of All Things* in 1621[24]. Paracelsus says "all natural forms bear their signatures, which indicate their true nature . . . This signature is often expressed in the exterior form of things, and by observing that form we may learn something in regard to their interior qualities . . . Plants used for the extraction of diseases bear the signature of the diseases"[83]. In addition to using herbs by the mouth Paracelsus used them to magnetically extract a disease by external application. In modern times these two forms of treatment were used by Rudolf Steiner, but the methods Steiner used were not only herbal; minerals and inorganic compounds were also employed. The idea now being put forward fits in very well with the Homoeopathic ideas, as well as with those put forward by Dr. A.T. Westlake in *The Pattern of Health*[225]. In this he describes a way of treating patients by using two or three dimensional patterns. From this developed the method of producing homoeopathic remedies from water treated by magnetically energised patterns. The references are given in the section on Homoeopathy, chapter 8, and Cymatics, chapter 9.

Finally herbs are considered to work by increasing the body's own natural resistance to disease. They help the body to throw off the disorder which is not itself attacked directly as in Allopathy. They do this through one or all of the three previously described ways.

Symptoms are still the main troubles that are treated. Some herbalists do not make a diagnosis nor rely on that made by an allopathic doctor in order to treat their patient. They give advice and treatment just like most medically orientated pharmacists. This is not as inexact a procedure as it may seem to an orthodox allopathic practitioner. The individual and his symptoms are the most important part of the diagnostic process. This will be obvious from reading the accounts of the other systems of therapy, especially Healing, Homoeopathy and Radiesthesia.

On the other hand there are herbalists of the highest professional standards and the school run by the National Institution of Medical Herbalists teaches all the basic sciences and pathology. Routine physical examination as well as modern allopathic diagnostic aids are used.

## Treatment

Herbal remedies are not toxic nor habit forming. They are administered by mouth as pills, capsules, juices and watery extracts, and externally as ointments. The remedies may be made of one, or several dried herbs ground into powder, or crude plants and roots from which infusions are made at home. Alternatively they may be bought professionally prepared from individual herbs and mixtures as in standard allopathic pharmaceutical practice. Natural vitamins are also used.

All these remedies are prescribed according to need, in conjunction with advice on correct living, diet, breathing and exercise. The aim is to improve the patient's resistance to disease, rather than to treat a specific disease.

## Governing Bodies

The National Institute of Medical Herbalists Ltd., 19 Cavendish Gardens, Barking, Essex. Founded in 1864, it runs an official Teaching School. It has 150 members.

The Society of Herbalists, 21 Bruton Street, London W1. Founded in 1928. It has 300 members.

## Comments

I have no personal experience of herbal remedies but I know many of my patients speak highly of them and I have been impressed by the herbalists I have met both as people of professional integrity and expertise. Allopathic medicine is missing out by its purist trend to use only single organic chemical compounds for treatment.

After the National Health Service began in 1948 there was a slump in Herbalism, but of recent years, in spite of having paid once for their health care, an increasing number of people are returning to the use of herbal remedies, which are far cheaper than allopathic medicines. Herbalism still has a considerable potential.

CHAPTER 8

# Homoeopathy

Dr Samuel Hahnemann, the Leipzig physician, developed Homoeopathy because he was horrified by the lethal side effects of the allopathic treatment of his time. His main work, *The Organon of Medicine* was first published in 1810 and ran to five editions in his life time [79]. Before him similar ideas were held by Dr Thomas Sydenham, Paracelsus. Hippocrates and are found in the even older Ayurveda of India, (chapter 11). In passing it is interesting to note that Hahnemann encountered most personal hostility from the pharmacists.

## Theory

There are two aspects to the theory of Homoeopathy. The first is summed up in the phrase "like cures like". The symptoms and physical signs — the sufferings of the patient — are considered to be a vigorous effort of the body to throw off the disease affecting it. That disease is an invisible thing. A fever and the germ associated with it should be regarded as the body's way of fighting the disease, not the result of the germ attacking the body. Therefore something which produces similar symptoms to the disease in a healthy body should help to deal with the disease producing those symptoms.

The opposite view is taken by Allopathy in which drugs are

used to block the chain of reactions of the body to the germ, or directly attack the germ itself. Yet Allopathy also uses immunisation where a small dose of a dead organism, or of an attenuated live organism, which causes a disease, is introduced into a body in order to raise its resistance to that disease. This is the principle on which Homoeopathy works. Clearly both views are correct and both can be effective ways of treatment. However, like immunisation, Homoeopathy corrects the disorder earlier in the chain of causation, yet produces less disturbance in doing so because it uses a new way of making therapeutic agents.

The second principle is that of the minimum dose. Hahnemann found that if he gave a normal big allopathic dose of one of his remedies to an ill person it produced a strong and disturbing effect. He began diluting his medicines and found that a very small dose would cure just as well without any upset for the patient. From this observation he developed the method of potentising remedies.

He found that by making greater and greater dilutions of his single medicines, they had increasingly powerful curative effects. These were increased if the drug and dilutent were ground together in a mortar if insoluble, or shaken in liquid if soluble. He considered it best for a physician to make his own remedies.

In the nineteenth century the relatively simple science of that time could not explain how Homoeopathy could work. People did not understand how a medicine which contained hardly any, or even no molecules of the remedy might have an effect.

Today we know that water is a giant molecule, and that it can receive and hold a message, through a re-arrangement in its pattern, by means of energy put into it — say for instance by shaking. In this shaking the pattern of the dissolved remedy is transmitted to the water. This pattern becomes more and more energised by each successive dilution and shaking, even though the number of molecules of the remedy becomes less and less[157 170].

Sister Justa Smith of Buffalo U.S.A.[177], has demonstrated that a healer, by placing his hands on a flask of digestive enzymes, can slow down their deterioration. Therefore an intention can be transmitted to a solution. This provides an explanation of Hahnemann's insistence that the physician, the person who wishes to heal his patient, should prepare the remedy himself.

All the water in a person's body is part of a giant molecule. Once the homoeopathic remedy has entered the patient's water its effect is exerted everywhere in the body. This explains the rapid action of high potency (very dilute, but much shaken), homoeopathic remedies.

### Diagnosis

This rests mostly on a very detailed history of the symptoms, a study of the type of person, both physically and mentally, age and sex. Hahnemann was insistent that careful notes should be taken of every symptom. Overall observation of the sick person is required, but no detailed physical examination is needed, but is usually done and may be helpful. Text books called Symptom Repertories relate the symptoms of the patient to the appropriate remedies.

### Treatment

There are about 2000 remedies, mostly single plants or portions of a plant, but also animal poisons, and some minerals.

If the substance selected as a remedy is soluble in water or alcohol a stock solution is made of either, or a mixture of the liquids. From this stock solution the remedies are prepared by two methods of dilution. The first is in steps of one in a hundred, that is one portion of stock solution to ninety nine parts of solvent, and shaken vigorously, which is called succussion. This is the first centesimal potency. One part of this potency is added to ninety nine parts of solvent and shaken again to make the second centesimal potency. This may be continued until the required strength is obtained, always taking one part of the preceding potency and ninety nine parts of solvent for the next. This scale is written as 1c, 2c etc., but as it is the most common the c is often omitted. The figure indicates the number of times the process of serial dilution has been carried out.

The second method is made in steps of one in ten, that is one portion of stock solution to nine portions of solvent. This is called the first decimal potency and is indicated by the letter X in Britain or D in Europe, thus 1X or 1D and this scale of potencies is always indicated in this way. The decimal potencies are seldom carried beyond the 30X. The process of potentising is exactly the same as for the centesimal scale.

If the preparation has to begin with an insoluble substance a portion of this is ground with a pestle in a mortar with ninety nine parts of lactose, making the first centesimal potency then one portion of this is ground with ninety nine more parts of lactose, and so on until after the 3C, the 4C can be made with alcohol, and the procedure continued as stated for potentisation by the liquid method. If the decimal system is used then one part of an insoluble substance is ground with nine parts of lactose and so on.

When the 30C potency is reached the remedy is exceedingly dilute. Such a remedy contains only one part in a figure which consists of 10 followed by 60 noughts; expressing this in logarithms the concentration is $10^{-60}$. At such a degree of dilution the remedy would be most unlikely to contain even one molecule from the original stock solution yet it would be homoeopathically effective.

The most commonly used potencies are the 6c, 12c, 30c, 200c and many prefer higher potencies still. The higher the potency the greater it's healing power because more energy for this purpose is available to be released at every stage.

The remedies are usually taken in the form of pure cane sugar pills into which the potentised liquid has been absorbed. Powders are also used in the same way, but liquid preparations are employed less often than either pills or powders.

Homoeopathic remedies can be obtained under the National Health Service on a doctors prescription from any pharmacist. The public can buy themselves homoeopathic remedies from pharmacists, within the statutory limits imposed by the Government on the sale of dangerous drugs. The only large manufacturing chemist of Homoeopathic remedies in the country supplies a set of "Nelson's Home Remedies". Dr Jack has written a brief pamphlet describing the use of these home remedies in general practice which is most informative[100].

The remedy which suits the most symptoms, the patient's age, sex and temperament is the first choice. The frequency of the dosage and the potency to use, is decided by experience from the nature of the symptoms, the type, age and sex of the patient. In practice for common illnesses and traumas a few dozen remedies suffice.

In many illnesses homoeopathy makes the patient whole if used properly. This is why so many questions are asked to get the "totality" of the illness of that unique sick individual. After influenza for instance, many homoeopathically treated patients say how well they feel, whereas patients treated with allopathic drugs uniformly say how weak and depressed they are.

Some acute illnesses may have to be followed by further constitutional treatment to rid the patient of the taint of obscure inherited tendencies which Hahnemann called Miasms. These tend to produce either recurrent varying acute diseases, or chronic disorders[2][179].

In the early stages of homoeopathic treatment there may be a temporary increase of symptoms, or another sort of disturbance, usually mild, before improvement sets in. This occurs seldom in acute disorders, and more often in long standing ones, especially those with an underlying miasm.

**Governing Body**

To become a homoeopathic practitioner it is necessary to qualify as a Registered Medical Pracitioner first. However, there are a number of practising lay Homoeopaths who are not doctors. Theirs is a difficult position, they have no standing and no society to which they can belong. Psionic, Radionic and Naturopathic practitioners also use homoeopathic remedies. There are only 127 homoeopathic doctors listed by the Homoeopathic Research and Educational Trust in 1974, and not all of these are practising Homoeopathy. These small numbers may well have resulted from the insistence of a prior medical qualification, adopted in order to ensure a high professional standard.

However, the materialising and emotionally blunting effect of brain washing during an allopathic training has to be experienced to be believed. It takes many years to recover from it. Most of its products never do so. Their conditioning is life long. This is why the recruitment of doctors to official Homoeopathy is so small.

The British Homoeopathic Association Inc., 27a Devonshire Street, London W1. The Membership of 1200 is open to all except lay homoeopathic practitioners. It exists to spread the knowledge and use of Homoeopathy. The journal *Homoeopathy* is published monthly.

The Faculty of Homoeopathy, Royal London Homoeopathic Hospital, Great Ormond Street, London W.C.1. This is the professional body for homoeopathic doctors, and governs training in Homoeopathy.

## Comments

My experience with Homoeopathy has been favourable, both personally and with patients. It works gently and often surprisingly quickly in acute disorders. However, one of Hahnemann's discoveries was his ability to use Homoeopathy to treat obscure inherited tendencies to chronic or recurrent acute diseases which he called miasms. These are the cause of many disorders which allopathy finds difficult to do more than suppress, since they are not self limiting.

The homoeopathic pharmacopoeia is exceptionally flexible, stable and comprehensive when compared with the gaps and constant changes in that of the allopathic system. The absence of side-effects and the simple indications for the use of about twenty remedies which cover most of the common ailments make Homoeopathy an admirable form of therapy for safe first aid and self medication.

Another advantage of Homoeopathy is that its mode of action lends itself readily for adaption to use in prevention, which allopathy does not because of its side effects. If its use for prophylaxis were combined with the predictive diagnostic possibilities of another system, like Radiesthesia (chapter 13), many advances would soon be made.

Homoeopathy is grossly underestimated as a system of treatment, and is rightly much used by Radionic (chapter 13), Osteopathic (chapter 5) and Naturopathic practitioners (chapter 10). In fact it would be fair to say that fewer homoeopathically medically qualified practitioners use homoeopathic remedies than those who are not so qualified.

Homoeopaths feel that slowly and surely the Medical (Allopathic) Establishment is trying to stifle their organisation. Recently the Government of South Africa has recognised Homoeopathy. It is hoped that the E.E.C. will do likewise for Homoeopathy is much more widely practised in Europe, where Homoeopathic remedies are mass produced on a large scale, and surely the community will not prevent its being taught or new homoeopaths being admitted to its territory as South Africa has done.

CHAPTER 9

# Miscellaneous

Bach Remedies, Biofeedback, Colour and Gem Therapy,
Cymatics, Magnetism, Orgone, Vita Florum.

## BACH REMEDIES

Edward Bach (1886–1936) was of Welsh stock. He qualified as a Registered Medical Practitioner in 1912, having trained at University College Hospital, London. He went on to take a diploma in Public Health, and became a bacteriologist to his old hospital where he taught students and published papers on original work in the field of bacterial immunology.[223]

When University College Hospital decided that their staff would be whole time he resigned and later became the Pathologist and Bacteriologist to the London Homoeopathic Hospital, where he soon found that he was in accord with Hahnemann's ideas. Further original work relating bacteriology to Homoeopathy followed, culminating in 1926 with his book *Chronic Disease: A Working Hypothesis* written in collaboration with Dr. C. E. Wheeler. He grew so busy that he gave up his post at the London Homoeopathic Hospital to run his own laboratories and a large practice.

His idea of treating chronic disease, then considered to be due to the influence of intestinal organisms, with oral homoeopathic doses of vaccines grown from cultures of the patient's stools and called "Bach Nosodes" did not wholly satisfy him, and he felt that the seven groups of bacteria he had isolated ought to be replaced by seven herbs.

The rest of his life was spent searching for herbal remedies. When this came into conflict with his practice he abandoned the latter even though at current money values it was bringing in about £30,000 a year, and he had not saved anything because he devoted all he had to research.

In the last years of his life he discovered 38 herbal remedies, wandering extensively over England and Wales to do so, as well as finding a few in Europe. These he tested on himself in the standard Homoeopathic way, suffering greatly from the often severe symptoms they induced for he was a frail and sensitive person.

He proved that sun warmed dew absorbed the properties of the plant on which it rested. It is interesting to note that dew collected at certain times forms the basis from which alchemical remedies are produced[7], but it is not known if Bach realised this. Since collecting sufficient dew from individual flowers was an impractical way of preparing remedies in quantity, he tried placing a few flowers from the selected plant in a glass bowl of pure spring water and left it standing in the field in full sunlight for a few hours.

This proved a potent way of impregnating the water with the power of a plant. The water is bottled and preserved with Brandy. These are the stock bottles. A few drops from these (usually five) are added to water in 1 oz. bottles from which the patient takes a few drops (again usually five) in a little water drunk one to three times a day.

A few remedies which need buds or some leaves and the stalk of the chosen plant are prepared by boiling in water for half an hour and then the stock solutions are prepared and taken as just described.

Bach wished everyone to realise and fulfil themselves by knowing and using his remedies. In 1931 he published *Heal Thyself – an explanation of the real cause and cure of disease*. It is a wise and inspiring book. *The Twelve Healers* followed in 1933, this was subsequently expanded to contain all his 38 herbal remedies. In order to spread his views, he advertised. For this he was duly warned by the General Medical Council, but strangely though he always maintained that he would continue to do so if he thought it necessary, and in spite of warning notices, he was never struck off the Medical Register for this defiance.

Bach prescribed his remedies for the patients' predominant emotional states, rather than their physical diseases, but the latter also responded. Personal experience and the use of Bach remedies on patients mainly with emotional difficulties has convinced me of their value. They work in the main on the homoeopathic principle of "Like cures like" (see chapter 8), stimulating the individual's defences against fear, depression and uncertainty, by innoculating him with a tiny dose of fear, depression and uncertainty. But a few convey a positive energy pattern which creates an improved emotional state directly in the way Vita Florum works as described later in this chapter.

I have kept a bottle of Bach's Rescue Remedy in my car and consulting rooms for 12 years, and give it when people collapse emotionally or physically. All the people treated recovered quickly after its use. I have also used the remedies occasionally for people with emotional problems, with success in four out of five cases. Personal use confirms their beneficial effect.

Dr. Edward Bach was the first to demonstrate that the healing power of plants could be transmitted to water by immersion alone, without solution and succussion as in homoeopathy, and also that plants need not work on the principle that like cures like, but can do so directly. For this, though he has been called the "Hahnemann of his time", he has not received the credit he deserves.

## BIOFEEDBACK

About ten years ago researchers began to ask the question whether a subject given information about the state of a function of his body, of which he was not normally aware, could learn to control that function. The answer proved to be yes, and the procedure was called biofeedback.

The method was a simple one of reward learning, already well known to animal trainers and also discussed in chapter 13 in the section on Behaviour Therapy. When the subject achieves a target such as lowering his blood pressure he is given a small reward in the form of an encouraging word, a sum of money or a sweet. If he is well motivated to succeed no reward other than the satisfaction of achievement is needed. A subject can learn to control many very delicate functions of which he is normally totally unaware, including those mediated through the subconscious, supposedly automatic self regulating part of the nervous system, called autonomic.

In the field of brain function a subject can learn to produce the alpha waves found in ordinary meditation and the theta waves associated with deeper meditation and psychic phenomena (see chapter 12). Groups who do this experience group psychic phenomena, such as telepathic exchanges of ideas and visions of each other. An epileptic child can be trained to reduce the frequency of the typical epileptic spiky waves with a reduction in the number of fits. In the field of meditation deep muscular relaxation can be achieved by connecting several muscles to a loud speaker which emits a bleep on the slightest muscular activity. By recording the skin resistance to a current, people can be trained to raise or lower this — raising it being an aid to relaxation and meditation.

In the field of cardiac and respiratory function people can be taught to raise or lower their blood pressure, pulse and breathing rate, all independently of each other. Patients with cold hands can learn to warm them. Patients with migraine, which is associated with arterial dilation in the head, can learn to reduce these attacks and by relaxing muscles at the back of the head reduce tension headaches. Rats have been taught to alter independently of each other, the length of various phases of an electrical recording of their heart beats (electrocardiographs — ECG for short). This is an incredibly swift adjustment involving small fractions of a second. Work is also being done on the application of a small computor, which estimates the volume of air breathed out in a minute from the rate of flow of air breathed out with each breath, to train asthmatics to control the degree of airway obstruction which constitutes their asthma.

Biofeedback methods can be used to help people who have had a stroke to regain their power of voluntary movement. In the normal state muscles are in a state of mild contraction. The action of a limb is achieved by some muscles which contract more and others which relax more. By connecting the muscles which contract more to perform a movement to a loud speaker, so that it sounds when they are in action, and the opposing group of muscles which ought to relax in order to allow the desired movement to occur, to another speaker which sounds only when they relax completely; a person who has received brain damage affecting the voluntary control of his muscles, such as a stroke, can have his recovery period greatly shortened by learning to make both speakers sound together while trying to perform the movement controlled by the two speakers. I have been told by those engaged in the work that people who have failed to recover on ordinary techniques have learnt to move again using the Biofeedback technique.

Biofeedback is a subject in which active research and expansion is taking place mainly in Japan and the U.S.A. where an annual digest of papers in the field is now published[20]. Without being too invasive of the body it should be possible to demonstrate many body functions instrumentally so that people can learn to control themselves. However it is not likely to be a replacement for other forms of therapy, though it will help considerably with some disorders, mainly those in the fields just mentioned, but especially in prophylaxis, and one can foresee a time when a simple course of basic biofeedback training will have a place in primary education.

This is important to educationalists because some of the mental states which are part of the process of learning can themselves be learnt by biofeedback techniques. It would also be relevant to mention here that meditative techniques also induce a capacity for learning as well as reducing a tendency to produce disturbance. For instance Transcendental Meditation is now taught in Canadian schools.

Though everyone can respond to Biofeedback training — not everyone is going to be a successful biofeedback athlete, and it is not likely to be a universal panacea. Nevertheless it is just in the field of learning to learn that it may have the most use — especially in combination with meditation and breathing exercises. I have found that by training people in the watch exercise[56], and certain yogic breathing exercises[155][156] then applying these for instance to making a cold hand warm, very successful. Whereas, when just faced with a thermometer and instructed to make the needle move in the direction of a higher temperature, little change occurred. Others have found a combination of autogenic training (chapter 12) and biofeedback useful for the same purpose.

However, the combination of yogic techniques which involve the manipulation of pre-physical Prana, Ch'i, or Ki (chapters 2, 5, 6, 12) raises the question of whether the Prana acts directly on the molecules of the part of the body to which it is mentally directed, or whether the change is mediated through the normal physiological channels as it is assumed to do in Biofeedback. Probably both actions occur one at one time, another at another, and when both together reinforcing each other the change takes place more readily. This is an interesting point, and has a bearing on the Nature of Healing (chapter 6), but it needs research.

## COLOUR AND GEM THERAPY

The Ancient Egyptians and Persians used Colour Therapy, but though there is ample scientific evidence that colour affects man both physically and mentally there is no use of it by the allopathic system of medicine today. Colour Therapy is conducted by anybody who has an interest in it.

Walter Birren, who is a colour consultant in the U.S.A., with an office in London, and whose colour code for safety has been internationally accepted, says:— "Two schools of thought, Mystics and Sceptics, are at loggerheads with each other, one making exaggerated and preposterous claims, and the other shouting denunciations of the entire business. In consequence a reasonable and fair attitude is overwhelmed. And Colour Therapy, humbly enough, must sit quietly by in the hope that tempers of men will one day grow sufficiently calm to enable them to prove the study of colour on a rational and impartial basis. Surely mankind would profit"[21].

This is a most reasonable assessment, not only of the situation of Colour Therapy but of the relationship of the allopathic system to all the other systems of therapy. It is a pity that very few specialists are as open minded as Walter Birren. His book *Colour Psychology and Colour Therapy* gives an excellent review and bibliography with only a few omissions.

In 1933 Dinshah Ghadiali, a Hindu, published *The Spectro-Chrometry Encyclopaedia* in three volumes. There is a good summary of this work by Mark Gallert in *New Light on Therapeutic Energies*[61]. Ghadiali made the point that colours represent chemical potencies in higher octaves of vibration which is in agreement with Steiner's views on the subject, as elaborated by Guenther Wachsmuth[212], though these are too divergent from the theme of this book to introduce here. An example of the relationship of chemical compounds to colour is found in the Spectrometry of burning elements, every one of which shows a characteristic dark line or lines at levels in its expanded spectrum. Furthermore the colour of the flame varies with the element being burned.

Ghadiali points out that all the colours in the spectrum exist in white light, and so long as pure spectral colours are used nothing foreign is added to the body. Yet in allopathic medicine this principle is ignored — "pouring into it (the body) many drugs containing elements not found in the body or in quantities far in excess of their natural portions in the body". "Chemicals are live potencies; their atoms have attractions and repulsions, and to endeavour to introduce haphazard inorganic metals into an organic machine, is like feeding a baby with steel tacks to make it strong." Colour Therapy leaves no harmful residues[65].

Ghadiali gives detailed instructions for the construction of lamps, which hues to use, what they do, and which are suitable for what conditions. He also mentions that water can be charged by exposing it to sunlight in a suitably coloured container. The water then takes on the characteristic action of the colour of the container when swallowed. This presumably works on the homoeopathic principle. Lactose (milk sugar) pills can be similarly charged.

This principle of charging water for internal use rather than exposing the patient to light baths on appropriate portions of his body saves time as well as elaborate equipment, and leads to two other forms of Colour Therapy appropriately mentioned here.

Firstly Gem Therapy described by B. Bhattacharyya[14]. Small good quality gems are left for a week in an alcoholic solution in the dark and then removed and stored for further use. Small lactose pills are soaked in the liquid and dried on white paper. These can now be given orally. The indications for treatment are broadly similar to those given by Ghadiali for Colour Therapy. Dr Bhattacharyya's son uses this method at his clinic in Naihati, Bengal, India.

Secondly Colour and Gem Therapy can be broadcast using radionic techniques (see chapter 13). This was first done in this country by David Tansley, who is a Chiropractor and a Radiesthetist[194], but is also done by Dr A. Bhattacharyya at his clinic, using a different method of broadcasting in which gems are spun or vibrated, so that the light from them, or the sound by which they are vibrated carries their characteristic colour to the patient through his witness, which in this method is a photograph or signature, though hair or a blood spot will do as well, placed in front of the gems.

An advantage of Gem Therapy is that only 9 gems are required. One for each colour of the spectrum, red, orange, yellow, green, blue, indigo and violet, and one each for ultra violet, and infra red. They can be small chips, but should be of good quality. In addition to lasting for ever, they are permanent true natural colours which do not fade, and that cannot be said of painted rooms and coloured slides.

The system of the Bhattacharyyas owes a lot to the work of Roland Hunt[92], but they have linked it to Ayurveda, to Homoeopathy, to Magnetism and Radiesthesia using a method of dowsing by magnet in a magnetic field which helps to eliminate errors, due to the varying capacities of individual dowsers and magnetic fields which change with the phases of the Moon[16 17].

Another system of Colour Therapy which is combined with Healing (see chapter 6), is for the therapist to select a strand of suitably coloured wool or silk for his patient's needs by intuition and to place it across the palm with the hand held facing towards the patient.

One further example of the importance of Colour is in personality testing. Most of the standard personality tests[172] such as the 16 Personality Factor Test are lengthy questionnaires which take from 2-3 hours to administer and do not give reliable results unless repeated more than once[33]. But the Luscher Personality Test, based on colour choices, is reliable on one performance, in fact it gives misleading results if repeated immediately, takes 7 minutes to administer and about 8 minutes to do a quick reading sufficient to give a comprehensive personality assessment. I have been using it for the last three years and remain most impressed by its efficiency and insights[134]. It is based on a combination of Kandinsky's[106] and Goethe's views on the emotional significance of colour[171].

One cannot help echoing Birren's summing up. Colour Therapy has indeed sat humbly by too long it is time it got lit up and signalled its coming of age.

## CYMATICS

In 1960, when the author was first trying to learn the clarinet, he was practising in the middle of a large field in Wales where the family caravan stood and a herd of about twenty cows were feeding. As is customary he was trying to do a descending scale of sustained notes. When he got down to bottom F all the cows came galloping towards him. As he was cut off from all sides, he stopped playing. The cows gathered around to stand in a respectful circle about twenty yards in diameter. Each time that F was repeated they moved a little closer, obviously interested, mostly with heads down, though a few of the more aesthetic ones held their heads on one side just like people enjoying a concert.

This practical example of Biocymatics — Cymatics[101] being the study of the relationship between waves and matter — demonstrates the effect of sound waves of a frequency of approximately 170½ cycles per second on the behaviour of Hereford Cows. It should not be taken too seriously, though it was exciting enough at the time it happened. What is significant is that sound produces patterns in sand spread on a thin metal plate as demonstrated by Ernest Chladni in the eighteenth century. The sand remains only on those parts of the plate where there is no vibration[220]. This point should be remembered as it is significant.

Hans Jenny has made it possible to demonstrate the effect of sound in three dimensions[102]. His "tonoscope" can be used with the human voice as the source of sound. When the sound for the letter 0 is spoken into the microphone a perfectly spherical pattern is produced. It is interesting to note that the symbol we have chosen to represent this sound is exactly the same shape that represents it in our script.

One then begins to wonder about the significance of sounds used in Mantra Yoga[69]. There is one sound which is said to be the seed sound of all things OM or AUM. The Hindu Mandukya Upanishad says "All that is, past — present and future — is truly OM. That which is beyond the triple conception of time is also OM"[15]. A similar interpretation of OM is found in Tibet among both Buddhists and Lamas, and in China, Japan and Indonesia.

Christians and Jews use AMEN, and the Muslims AMIN. The idea that sound conditions form is ancient and widespread in many cultures. This concept was old when the Gospel according to St John, which starts "in the beginning was the word" was written, and still not new when the walls of Jericho came down to the sound of trumpets.

The Ancient Egyptians understood the relationship of form and substance to tone. "The tradition of the Egyptians indicates to us in many ways, each independent of the other, that the two colossal statues of Memnon in the Valley of the Nile gave forth every morning a tone at sunrise and greeted thus" the rising of the sun[213]. I.H. Brested says in his "History of Egypt" "Only the two weather-beaten Colossi still look out across the plain; one of them still bearing the scribblings in Greek of curious tourists in the time of the Roman Empire who came to hear the marvellous voice which issued from it every morning at sunrise"[25].

Wachsmuth, who was a pupil of Rudolf Steiner (chapter 4) goes on to say that the forms of the statues had so weathered down that they had lost their original form and are silent today. He considers sound to be the chemical ether of the four ethers or formative forces — the others being Life, Warmth and Light. The ethers are precursors of the physical, and should be regarded as similar to Ki, Ch'i or Prana. The sound ether is a suctional force drawing inward and tending to produce condensation of substance. The phenomenon of tone arises when, and at the point where, conflict begins between the chemical and light ethers over substance for its rarefication or condensation. This is the reason why sound produced in a vacuum is not propagated. Sound only occurs when conflict can take place between the light and chemical ethers. In a space void of air there is no substance for conflict[214].

In modern times in the west, though there is evidence that sound affects health adversely[221], there is no therapeutic use of sound, though experiments on plant growth indicate plants exposed to music grow better than those left to the random noise of everyday life[207][228].

In India B. Bhattacharyya states that healing mantras may be written on a piece of paper, preferably in red, and transmitted as in colour therapy either by vibration or rotation[18]. Mantras are also used in Ayurveda, see chapter 11.

In *All and Everything* George Gurdjieff gave an account of the laws of sound[74]. He mentioned the use of specially tuned modern grand pianos to produce and cure a boil. Nothing Gurdjieff has written is without meaning. He mentioned that when he wrote that there were no instruments which could be used to record rates of vibration of musical notes. This is not the case now, so we have the possibility of studying the therapeutic influence of sound.

Here must be one of the projects of future research. For sound is rapid in action, and easily and cheaply applied.

Up to now the effect of sound vibrations upon matter have been under consideration — that is the influence of vibration upon form. We must now turn to the reverse process the influence of form upon vibrations. Here a static pattern influences vibrations which are proceeding in and around it. As in Chladni and Jenny's observations the process can be two or three dimensional.

It is well known that certain buildings influence people who are in them. For instance, Chartres and Notre Dame Cathedrals in France, The Blue Mosque in Istanbul and Ulu Cami (The Great Mosque) in Bursa, the old capital of the Ottoman Empire, the Taj Mahal in India and the Great Pyramids in Egypt[27] have a profound effect on those who remain in them for some time. I can vouch for the influence of the first four. I always revisit Chartres whenever possible and one day hope to stay some time in Bursa. The Great Mosque there affected me deeply — I wept as I was induced to worship there.

The secrets of the proportions of these buildings must have been passed down as part of the craft secrets of the mediaeval masons. Recently some of the principles involved have been worked out by Jay Hambidge[78] and Matila Ghyka[66][67]. The golden mean ratio of 1 to 1.618 can be easily used by simple geometric constructions to produce a growing series of harmonious spatial relationships. This idea was developed in modern times by Le Corbusier who worked out his modulor system based on the size of the average man with his arm raised using the same principles and applied them in architecture[124]. Once one gets used to the idea it is easy to pick out at a glance a building whose designer was using the golden mean in dynamic harmony as opposed to static harmony.

The principle is one of logarithmic growth, giving an equiangular spiral such that any line drawn from its centre makes a constant angle with a tangent to the curve. All growing things increase in size according to this principle which is most easily demonstrated in plants[208][108], shells[37][204] and crystallography[68]. In life, as in architecture, the principle of dynamic harmony allows something to grow while its original shape and proportions remain constant.

The Ancient Egyptians, as mentioned previously, and subsequently the Greeks understood the principle — hence their beautiful buildings and sounding statues. But there is another aspect to be considered. About 50 years ago a Frenchman, M. Bovis, observed that small animals that had died in the Great Pyramid did not decay, but instead became mummified despite the humidity.

Pondering over this a Czech engineer connected it with the observation that the polarised light from the moon blunted razor blades, and wondered if the preservative action of a model pyramid might not have the reverse effect. It did, provided the original proportions and orientation of the pyramid were preserved, and the blade placed centrally in the model pyramid one third of the way up with the sharp edges facing east to west. The sceptical Czech patent office proved its efficiency and the Cheops Pyramid Razor Blade Sharpener was launched[145].

Ostrander and Schroeder mention other examples of the action of form − shape − or pattern on living things. The French yogurt manufacturer who patented a special container because it increased the action of the germ which changed the milk. A change in the shape of beer containers from round barrels to rectangular shapes made it taste worse. Mice with identical wounds heal faster if kept in spherical cages, and schizophrenic patients improve if they live in trapezoidally shaped hospital wards[145].

In the section on Radionics, chapter 13, it is mentioned that Malcolm Rae has demonstrated that homoeopathic remedies can be prepared from water using magnetically energised patterns. The patterns Rae used were derived from those produced by a small research group organised by Dr A.T. Westlake between 1954 and 1957 using the technique of question and answer using the radiesthetic faculty (see chapter 13) he describes the method and results in detail in his book *The Pattern of Health* and in the second edition gives some of the patterns they worked out[225].

There are three static patterns with a ratio of 1 to 3 in which the forces move centrifugally and require the operator's protection, and dynamic patterns based on a ratio of 2 to 5 with a centrifugal movement with which the operator needs no protection. At points on the pattern Bach, or Homoeopathic remedies are placed with a patient's witness at the centre, for a radiesthetically determined period of time. The static patterns need actual remedies, the dynamic patterns only the name of the remedy written in the right positions.

Eventually the group derived a master pattern of the various levels of a living being's organisation from the chemical level at the periphery inwards through the plant, animal, emotional and mental to the spiritual. They found that one of the connecting links between all the diagrams was colour, and that it was possible to give the exact shade the patient needed by means of the diagrams, whereas this is difficult with modern transparent films which fade.

Nearly 300 cases were treated with good results but the use of the patterns has not been explored, except by Malcolm Rae as already mentioned, where the emphasis has been on the production of the homoeopathic remedies which work by the vaccination principle of a relatively harmless noxious stimulus to the defence mechanisms rather than an increase in the natural defences of the body or a direct action for good against the invading agent which might well be possible if the pattern was suitably orientated.

Here is another aspect of cymatics which seems to present a wide open field for a major advance in therapeutic methods. The patterns need not be three dimensional. A photographic reproduction of the key diagram could be used to produce easily mass produced therapeutic machines for use by a small group such as a family to treat its illnesses under instruction from a practitioner who would only need to determine the need of the sick person radiesthetically from his witness (see chapter 13).

It is well established that waves influence solids, and enough has been written to indicate that the opposite also holds. A form or shape which can be reduced to a pattern can influence vibrations taking place around or in its sphere of activity. A study of these relationships, including the influence of magnetic fields upon the cymatic situation, would be very enlightening for the biological sciences especially its therapeutic division. It seems quite likely that if the Radiesthetic phenomenon was studied from these aspects new light would be thrown upon its, at present mysterious, way of working and upon how healing works.

## MAGNETISM

This is a method of therapy of which the author has neither personal experience, nor has he been able to talk to an active practitioner and patients who have had experience of the treatment. However, recent developments such as the manufacture of plastic magnetic strips that make the application of treatment much easier, and the discovery of a particle representing the basic unit of magnetism, called a monopole because of its single polarity, at Berkeley University, California, USA, and the universal distribution of magnetism which has been neglected as an influential agent by the biological sciences, are all factors which led to its inclusion here[141].

Magnetism was used by the ancient Egyptians and Greeks. Paracelsus described the use of magnets in treatment from several angles[85]. Reichenbach and Mesmer employed it in the eighteenth century, but after this the trend of medical science set in the direction of chemistry, and it is almost entirely in the domain of biochemistry that the nature of life and disease has been studied in the past century.

Though the influence of magnetic fields on all forms of organic life has been neglected, there have been many recent observations of the effect of moon cycles on plant growth, animal and human behaviour as well as the influence of equinoctial changes on chemical reactions[109][87], and there have been people who realised that the probable agent was magnetism[208]. There have also been others who have studied the effects of magnetic fields on living things. Davis and

Bhattacharyya[39] and Madeline Barnothy[10] have done so, and written books on the subject. S.W. Tromp did an able review of the literature up to 1961[209].

Rodney Collin in *The Theory of Celestial Influence*[36] pointed out that the mass and spiral passage of the planets through space made them vast electromagnets and cited many examples of cyclic events which correlated with the movements of planets and other solar systems. His ideas correlate with the work of Gauquelin, see chapter 7 on Herbalism[64].

Davis has been able to make a colour photograph of the magnetic flux from the South Pole of a magnet towards the north using a flat hollow circular disc of glass, with the air pumped out to form a vacuum tube about a quarter of an inch thick. Both sides of the glass are treated with phosphorus. This tube serves for observation of the magnetic lines that appear when electronic beams are fired into the tube, while it is placed close to one pole of the magnet. The lines are about 20 to the inch. Those from the South Pole spin clockwise and those from the North Pole spin anticlockwise. Possibly the separate particles called monopoles make up the lines of flux and exert their influence from the direction of rotation, and flow from the South to the North Pole.

In magnetic therapy the action of the South Pole is, as would be expected from the above, expansive − it says "go" to the tissues. The action of the North Pole is to contract or to stop. This reads like the far eastern description of the Yin and the Yang (see chapters 2, 5 and 11). It becomes even more like it when one remembers that the lines of magnetic flux run from the South on an ovoid course to the North Pole of a bar magnet, changing their polarity at the equator for, at extremes the Yin turns into the Yang and vice versa.

Furthermore Yin attracts Yang, but Yin and Yin and Yang and Yang repel each other, just like North and South magnetic poles. This raises the question, are Yin and Yang manifestations of magnetism? If so what is K'i the force that is transformed into them? Is it unpolarised magnetism?

From instructions on meditation[51][69], and Tai Chi (chapter 5) we learn that Ki (Ch'i or Prana) can be manipulated by thought and we arrive at the position which suggests that if we set about it the right way mental activity can change the form of a living body. For if magnetism influences life, which it seems to, and magnetism is polarised energy (Ki, Ch'i or Prana) which influences living things, and it can be directed by mental activity which is said to happen, then we have the proposition that matter influences mind and mind influences matter which is the basis of the quotation from the *Mahabharata* at the end of chapter 1. It also fits in with Hindu and Tibetan, Theosophic and far eastern Zen Buddhist ideas.

Apart from applying the North or South Pole of a bar magnet, or taping a plastic magnet on to the part to be treated, water in which the appropriate pole has been dipped becomes polarised, but not magnetised, and can be used either to influence plant growth or treat disease. North polarised water makes plants grow tall, and South pole polarised water shorter and bushier. Polarised water can also be used to treat diseases, and a case of cholecystitis is quoted by Dr R.U. Sierra. Here is another example of how water can carry a pattern and transmit it to a patient as in Homoeopathy (see chapter 8, and in this chapter see Bach remedies, Colour Therapy and Vita Florum). Dr Sierra also quotes cases of cancer with widespread secondaries, cerebral atheroma, and generalised arthritis who had been given up by their medical practitioners, but who responded well to magnetic therapy, involving the direct application of one pole of a bar magnet over the affected areas of the body[176].

One more possibility of biomagnetism is worth mentioning. Rats exposed to bipolar fields of increased power — say 600

...lso be made.

...ake has used a 3 fold box accumulator with a flexible ... or the treatment of burns, and wounds where it ... pain and produces rapid healing without scars. I ... personal experience of this accumulator using it to ... area of synovitis of the knee which had been painful ... days. A cool sensation was felt, and after ½ an hour ... went. It did not return.

...eveloped a theory of the development of cancer using ... powered magnifications (x2 — 3,000) of unstained ...ssues. The usual research methods are of dead stained ...t magnifications of about 1,000. He concluded that ... arose in areas of the body where for psychological ... there have been spasms and inhibitions which prevent ... flow of Orgone. The invasive cancer cell is a product ...defence mechanism of the body against the cellular ... and breakdown that the spasms and inhibitions ...ver long periods of time induce. Once the invasive ...ell is produced the process is self perpetuating.

...a very concise summary of his theory. It fits with the ... tendency of cancer to occur in certain emotional ...ith its invasiveness, and with modern idea that cancer ... to a breakdown of the body's defence mechanisms ... cancer cells which are always being produced in older

...treated cases of cancer with daily irradiations in an ... accumulator, and reported shrinking of the tumors ...provements in weight and strength. However he ...red that when established cancer was present the ...nt was bound to have a limited effect, and that the ...ge of his theory of cancer and orgone therapy, lay in ...lity to detect precancerous changes early and treat

gauss instead of the half gauss the earth gives us — lived much longer than mice who live in similar conditions but only in the Earth's natural field. However, they become dependent on the artificially powerful magnetic field and die rapidly if this is cut off[176].

Sister Justa Smith who demonstrated that a healer can slow down the rate of deterioration of enzymes, has also shown that very strong magnetic fields of 5-6,000 Gauss do the same[178]. There is also evidence that magnetic fields influence the growth of plants. This and the healing aspects of magnetism are discussed in the *Secret Life of Plants*[208]. References to the subject are starting to appear in text-books of plant physiology, but the authors are cautious, pointing out that there has been insufficient study for critical analysis[19]. One piece of research showing the influence of a magnetic field on the growth of roots was done by L.J. Audus as long ago as 1960[5].

It is hoped that enough has been said to stimulate interest in biomagnetic therapy, because the agent used is cheap to produce and easily applied.

## ORGONE

Wilhelm Reich 1897-1957 was one of Freud's brightest pupils but quarrelled with him shortly after the publication of Reich's book, *The Function of the Orgasm*[159]. This was not surprising, for Freud was puritanical about sex; this could not be said of Reich, who was a brilliant and original psychotherapist, thinker, author and scientist, but had the capacity for arousing hostility and becoming a martyr wherever he went.

During his relatively short and stormy life Reich wandered from Vienna to Berlin, Sweden, Norway and finally in 1934 to the U.S.A., where he died insane from a myocardial infarct in a Federal Penitentiary serving a two year sentence for failure to obey an injunction obtained by the Food and Drug Administration (FDA)[233].

This injunction was extraordinary, for it enjoined the defendants "from distribution of Orgone Energy containers ... all accumulators to be disassembled ... all printed matter regarding these or orgone energy to be destroyed", *on the grounds that orgone energy does not exist,* and therefore was "misbranded and adulterated"[35]. Yet no research upon the instrument had been conducted by the FDA.

If it did not exist why bother, why no research when Reich had experimented for years, and why the severity? For not only were he and the Director of the Orgone Institute imprisoned, and the Institute heavily fined, but the whole of his work and scientific papers were as far as possible incinerated. Perhaps the clue lies in the horrific account of the ill fated Oranur Experiment described by Reich[160].

In December 1950 an experiment went wrong and a reaction between orgone and Radium occurred. This led to the mass death of the Orgone's Institute experimental mice, and radiation sickness of the research workers who survived thanks to Reich's able handling of the situation. But the background radiation count for 600 miles around was raised and this probably drew too much attention to the Institute's activities.

However, arising out of these events a way could have been developed of countering the effects of radiation, or even providing a new source of energy. Reich had now discovered Deadly Orgone (DOR). This is an initial reaction of Orgone to nuclear fission. It was noticed that clouds of DOR were increasing in the atmosphere, probably due to the increased number of atomic explosions releasing nuclear material to react with naturally occurring Orgone which is a life sustaining force.

Reich thought that the lack of rain was a result of DOR in excess, and dispersed rain would fall. He was w good results when his appeal agains and he was arrested for contempt of co was then ruthlessly applied (see chapt

Reich's main book is *The Discovery* he incorporated as a first part, the *F* The second part — *The Cancer Biop* nature and reaction of orgone, which pre-material cosmic energy, a source mary of his work by Mark Gallert[6] A.T. Westlake[226], and long extracts in h

To give the principles very briefly, penetrating everything though at dif electro-magnetic; organic material ho then repel it quickly. It flows fro concentrations of itself, unlike kine and species has a certain capacity for the surplus. It moves always in wave general from east to west. It transm speed of light and in contact with an Reich also stated it had a motor force.

From the responses of metal and orga it is possible to construct an accumula box made of alternate layers of meta with metal on the inside. Since the from the outside of the metal it accu then be directed by a flexible tube lec to an area outside the box. The pow can be increased by making the numb ting layers greater. Large accumulators

For this reason, and also because it kept him in good health and full of energy, he always kept himself highly charged with Orgone. Perhaps this is why he became paranoid and died of a coronary heart disease when deprived of regular supplies of Orgone in prison. Maybe like Dr. Sierra's unfortunate rats who died when deprived of the high powered magnetic field in which they were accustomed to live, he too had become habituated to Orgone and suffered the physical effects of its withdrawal.

Wilhelm Reich, though he died about as discredited as anyone can be, left a memorial of highly significant psychological work. His views on sex and body armour broke new ground, and make good sense. His writings on life and politics have recently been republished, and are of interest. Perhaps his scientific work is of the same order. Certainly they need a thorough and sympathetic reassessment [161] [162] [163].

## VITA FLORUM

The name sounds like a Roman advertisement for flower power, but the product is backed by an impressive stack of testimonials from satisfied users, and I can vouch personally for its effectiveness in curing an intractible patch of eczema, and as a treatment for household burns. The ointment also healed two raw areas on the hands of a farmer who has been unsuccessfully treated for two years by his doctors.

A selection of flowers, some rare, and some from Southern Europe are listed on the containers of the product, water in which they have been dipped. The flowers are not picked as in the manufacture of Bach remedies, but simply held in sunlight, in water, till their power passes into it. In this respect they work on the principle Edward Bach discovered.

On the other hand, unlike the majority of the Bach remedies

they do not work on the homoeopathic principle of like curing like. Elizabeth Bellhouse who chose the flowers intuitively, through her ability to communicate with plants[229] calls her remedies Homoeovitic Potencies to distinguish their action from the homoeopathic. She says "Homoeopathic means having the same base as illness; "Homoeovitic" means having the same base as vitality or life"[11].

This is a new principle. She thinks that her potentised selection of flowers are the radiations of the Creator as emitted by the flowers, and radiate into the person that takes them or applies them to his body. This allows the whole man to develop harmoniously and the disharmonies which constitute disease and psychic disturbances disappear. Rudolf Steiner's description of the divisions of plants is consistent with this view. Flowers are the reproductive, radiating parts of plants (chapter 4).

Elizabeth Bellhouse has been working on these remedies for the past twenty years. She says some profound things — for instance . . . "Matter is so wholly, infinitely and at every second, transmutable as to the quantity, the location, and the mode of its manifestation in three dimensions, that it can quite correctly be said; matter has no true existence of its own. In reality all matter is a happening, which as to quality manifests in accordance with the quality reigning in mens' hearts"[12].

In commenting on the significance of the fall of man she says . . . "When Adam decided to do his own thing rather than play the part he was designed to play in the creation set up, (his action was) analgous to a car's steering wheel deciding it would revolve as the road wheels do, rather than serve in the capacity for which it was designed and intended. The result was a forgone conclusion; the whole of creation went beserk"[13]. This is a clear example of the operation of the Jack Principle (chapter 1).

gauss instead of the half gauss the earth gives us — lived much longer than mice who live in similar conditions but only in the Earth's natural field. However, they become dependent on the artificially powerful magnetic field and die rapidly if this is cut off[176].

Sister Justa Smith who demonstrated that a healer can slow down the rate of deterioration of enzymes, has also shown that very strong magnetic fields of 5-6,000 Gauss do the same[178]. There is also evidence that magnetic fields influence the growth of plants. This and the healing aspects of magnetism are discussed in the *Secret Life of Plants*[208]. References to the subject are starting to appear in text-books of plant physiology, but the authors are cautious, pointing out that there has been insufficient study for critical analysis[19]. One piece of research showing the influence of a magnetic field on the growth of roots was done by L.J. Audus as long ago as 1960[5].

It is hoped that enough has been said to stimulate interest in biomagnetic therapy, because the agent used is cheap to produce and easily applied.

## ORGONE

Wilhelm Reich 1897-1957 was one of Freud's brightest pupils but quarrelled with him shortly after the publication of Reich's book, *The Function of the Orgasm*[159]. This was not surprising, for Freud was puritanical about sex; this could not be said of Reich, who was a brilliant and original psychotherapist, thinker, author and scientist, but had the capacity for arousing hostility and becoming a martyr where-ever he went.

During his relatively short and stormy life Reich wandered from Vienna to Berlin, Sweden, Norway and finally in 1934 to the U.S.A., where he died insane from a myocardial infarct in a Federal Penitentiary serving a two year sentence for failure to obey an injunction obtained by the Food and Drug Administration (FDA)[233].

This injunction was extraordinary, for it enjoined the defendants "from distribution of Orgone Energy containers ... all accumulators to be disassembled ... all printed matter regarding these or orgone energy to be destroyed", *on the grounds that orgone energy does not exist,* and therefore was "misbranded and adulterated"[35]. Yet no research upon the instrument had been conducted by the FDA.

If it did not exist why bother, why no research when Reich had experimented for years, and why the severity? For not only were he and the Director of the Orgone Institute imprisoned, and the Institute heavily fined, but the whole of his work and scientific papers were as far as possible incinerated. Perhaps the clue lies in the horrific account of the ill fated Oranur Experiment described by Reich[160].

In December 1950 an experiment went wrong and a reaction between orgone and Radium occurred. This led to the mass death of the Orgone's Institute experimental mice, and radiation sickness of the research workers who survived thanks to Reich's able handling of the situation. But the background radiation count for 600 miles around was raised and this probably drew too much attention to the Institute's activities.

However, arising out of these events a way could have been developed of countering the effects of radiation, or even providing a new source of energy. Reich had now discovered Deadly Orgone (DOR). This is an initial reaction of Orgone to nuclear fission. It was noticed that clouds of DOR were increasing in the atmosphere, probably due to the increased number of atomic explosions releasing nuclear material to react with naturally occurring Orgone which is a life sustaining force.

Reich thought that the lack of rain which produces deserts was a result of DOR in excess, and if these clouds could be dispersed rain would fall. He was working in Arizona with good results when his appeal against the injunction failed, and he was arrested for contempt of court. The "Best Defence" was then ruthlessly applied (see chapter 1).

Reich's main book is *The Discovery of the Orgone* in which he incorporated as a first part, the *Function of the Orgasm.* The second part — *The Cancer Biopathy* — deals with the nature and reaction of orgone, which he considered to be a pre-material cosmic energy, a source of life. There is a summary of his work by Mark Gallert[62], a shorter version by A.T. Westlake[226], and long extracts in his selected writings[160].

To give the principles very briefly, Orgone is everywhere, penetrating everything though at different speeds. It is not electro-magnetic; organic material holds it; metals attract it, then repel it quickly. It flows from weaker to stronger concentrations of itself, unlike kinetic energy. Each thing and species has a certain capacity for Orgone and discharges the surplus. It moves always in waves, or pulsations, and in general from east to west. It transmits its energy with the speed of light and in contact with an atmosphere luminates. Reich also stated it had a motor force.

From the responses of metal and organic material to Orgone it is possible to construct an accumulator. This consists of a box made of alternate layers of metal and organic material with metal on the inside. Since the Orgone cannot escape from the outside of the metal it accumulates inside and can then be directed by a flexible tube led from the space inside to an area outside the box. The power of the accumulator can be increased by making the number of layers of alternating layers greater. Large accumulators in which a subject can sit may also be made.

Dr Westlake has used a 3 fold box accumulator with a flexible outlet for the treatment of burns, and wounds where it relieves pain and produces rapid healing without scars. I have had personal experience of this accumulator using it to treat an area of synovitis of the knee which had been painful for a few days. A cool sensation was felt, and after ½ an hour the pain went. It did not return.

Reich developed a theory of the development of cancer using very high powered magnifications (x2 — 3,000) of unstained living tissues. The usual research methods are of dead stained tissues at magnifications of about 1,000. He concluded that cancer arose in areas of the body where for psychological reasons there have been spasms and inhibitions which prevent the free flow of Orgone. The invasive cancer cell is a product of the defence mechanism of the body against the cellular swelling and breakdown that the spasms and inhibitions acting over long periods of time induce. Once the invasive cancer cell is produced the process is self perpetuating.

This is a very concise summary of his theory. It fits with the known tendency of cancer to occur in certain emotional states, with its invasiveness, and with modern idea that cancer is due to a breakdown of the body's defence mechanisms against cancer cells which are always being produced in older people.

Reich treated cases of cancer with daily irradiations in an Orgone accumulator, and reported shrinking of the tumors and improvements in weight and strength. However he considered that when an established cancer was present the treatment was bound to have a limited effect, and that the advantage of his theory of cancer and orgone therapy, lay in the ability to detect precancerous changes early and treat them.

Vita Florum comes as a fluid for internal use, with a lotion and ointment for external application. There are also veterinary and agricultural preparations. It is hoped that a properly conducted trial, that will allow its effectiveness to be scientifically assessed will not be long delayed. It is important to do this because a diagnosis is not necessary before using Vita Florum. It is claimed to work on everybody and everything, as a general tonic and in more frequent doses as a therapeutic agent. If this were proved to be true it might really be the "Magic Bullet" — the therapeutic cure all, that Erlich sought in the chemical field, and everybody else has also failed to find. Yet it would be much more than this, for it should not be regarded as a medicine, but as a harmonising agent that opens the way for psychological and spiritual growth, and consequently heals. It puts first things first.

CHAPTER 10

# Naturopathy

People prefer unhealthy indoor lives, eating extensively without discrimination denatured foods containing chemical additives, taking drugs, including alcohol and tobacco, and striving after absurd aims. It is not surprising they ignore the naturopathic approach, even though they need it greatly.

At the turn of the nineteenth century Naturopathy developed out of Hydrotherapy as an approach to ill health. It was based on the idea that any disturbance in the harmony of nature resulted in disorder. Hence the term Naturopathy derived as are Homoeopathy and Allopathy.

### Theory

The Naturopath tries to find the primary disturbance in the organism before the signs or symptoms of the 'dis-ease' appear. A true corrective treatment must be related to conditions which preceded the symptoms, and even though they no longer exist, they can be determined.

Illnesses are regarded as constructive. Colds, fevers, infections and rashes are seen as readjustments of the body which is getting rid of its disharmony — unpleasant certainly, but useful. If such illnesses are obstructed by interfering with the process, chronic disease tends to develop.

Naturopathy is better applied prophylactically to maintain health. "We do not offer to cure our patients, our work is essentially educational . . . Naturopathy is demanding of the patient." It is a way of life similar to that of oriental therapy [205].

**Practice**

Fasting, diet and alterations in the patient's way of life play the largest part in the system. Manipulation, and hydrotherapy are parts of its armamentarium. There is an acceptance of the need for surgery of wounds, fractures, obstructive and congenital lesions. Massage and posture correction are also employed.

The purist approach is that "Naturopathy is not . . . a substitute for medication. It cannot be produced in doses for specific ailments"[205]. However, people do not usually consult practitioners of any persuasion before they feel ill, and always demand relief from their symptoms as quickly as possible. Inevitably therefore, because their basic ideas combine well with some other systems of therapy, many Naturopaths practice more than one discipline. In particular, osteopathy and acupuncture are used, but some also use herbal and homoeopathic remedies. Natural vitamins and minerals are also employed just as in chiropractic and osteopathy.

**Governing Bodies**

The purists are represented by the Incorporated Society of Registered Naturopaths, Kingston, Edinburgh. Founded in 1927, it requires 4 years full time training in a school whose standards are recognised by the Society. Its members put after their names, only the words Registered Naturopath, and confine the use of initials to state recognised degrees. No member of the society may prescribe remedies or use hypnotism. The 'true blue' Naturopath believes that what is wrong with his patient can be cured by fasting and diet alone. The Society has 30 members, 19 of whom are in practice. There is a 40 bedded hospital in Edinburgh.

The pragmatic approach is represented by the British Naturopathic and Osteopathic Association, 6 Netherall Gardens, London NW3. It was founded in 1925. This association allows Naturopaths to mix therapies as mentioned previously, permits the use of initials of the Society as a qualification after members' names, and has a three year course of training before admission. There are about 200 Naturopaths who hold the pragmatic approach. The majority belong to the BNOA, but from time to time breakaway associations form.

### Comments

I have no personal experience of Naturopathy.

It seems to have a sound approach that should underly everyone's way of life. We should all live naturopathically, yet this situation places naturopathy at a disadvantage. People are disinclined to change their habits and live in this way. They wait till they feel ill, then they demand treatment, so naturopaths in order to survive, have to swallow their ideals and treat sick people. Naturopathy is in danger of gradually merging into other systems which treat diseases after they can be recognised, and gradually loosing its identity.

It would be a pity to lose the considerable body of knowledge of the effects of wrong eating, and sound dietary ideas which have been slowly accumulated by Naturopaths, some of whom are seeing success in chronic disorders by such treatment. Some cases of cancer seem to respond to naturopathic measures (see also chapter 11). Nevertheless, not even by stretching one's imagination to the utmost, can it be conceived that all diseases are cured by diet and fasting only.

CHAPTER 11

# Oriental Therapy

History, Ayurveda, Far Eastern, Tibetan.

Oriental therapy is ancient, estimates vary from three to five thousand years. It originated probably in the Nile and Euphrates Valleys' civilisations which were roughly contemporary, though the estimates of the age of the Ancient Egyptian civilisation usually make it out to be a little older than the Sumerian. However it must be admitted that we do not know whether there were contemporary civilisations in Tibet and China at the times when the ancient Egyptians and Sumerians flourished, though the lateness of the stone age in China suggests that this is unlikely in that country.

Since ancient Egyptian and Sumerian medicine has not survived, they need not be discussed, nor will ancient Greek medicine, not only for the same reason, but also because it is most likely that the Greeks obtained many of their ideas from Sumerian, Egyptian and Indian sources.

The idea that western medicine had Greek origins is a Renaissance scholars' notion, true enough as an immediate source of transmission, but not able to stand up to a wider view of history, and wider linguistic knowledge. Professor Cyril Elgood, a medical historian, writes — "The so called Greek views had been taught long before on the banks of the

Euphrates, and before that in India"[47]. Sir William Jones says — "Hindu medical classics . . . do not contain a single technical term which points to foreign origin"[103], whereas the opposite cannot be said about Greek Literature where not only the ideas, but also many of the drugs listed in the pharmacopaeia are of Middle Eastern and Indian origin[113].

The question of the origins of Greek medicine is discussed at length by Dr P. Kutumbiah who points out that Hippocrates derived his doctrine of the four humours from Alcmaeon who belonged to the school of Pythagoras[114]. Now Pythagoras was trained in Egypt but taken as a captive to Babylon by Cambyses. He spent many years there and no doubt became acquainted with Sumerian and Indian ideas[94]. This view is upheld by Hopkins, who says "We are unable to come to any other conclusion than that this philosopher (Pythagoras) took his whole system indirectly from India"[88].

However it is not possible to go along with Kutumbiah's view that while the similarities between the Greek and Indian systems are superficial, the differences are fundamental[115]. Where ideas have a common origin they must be basically similar. Wherever ideas arise in the world, they arise in man from the infinite. There is an underlying unity in everything. Every alternative has a meaning, to discard any apparently discordant idea is to lose a part of the whole from which it came.

Around 2500 BC there was a Bronze Age civilisation with well developed art and architecture, but whose writings on stone and metal remain undeciphered, in the Indus Valley. About 1500 BC there was an invasion of Aryans from the north over the mountains of the Hindu Kush. The resulting civilisation spread over India mixing with the Dravidians who then, as now, lived in Southern India, and from it came, about 1200 BC, the earliest Hindu sacred writings — the Rig-Veda, Sama-Veda, Yajur-Veda and Atharva-Veda.

The Hindus believe that these scriptures were taught by gods to sages, or revealed to sages who were seers of truth. This would fit in with suggestions made here and there, that there have been civilisations which perished though they left remnants in periodic cataclysms which changed the geography of the earth, and that civilisation on earth is much older than orthodox archeologists wish us to think [110] [206].

Veda means "knowledge" or "science", and Atharva means "priest-physician". This implies an organisation similar to that of the ancient Egyptians — so that the Indo-Aryans seem to have had a ready-made philosophical and therapeutic system from the time of their earliest records. Ayurveda — the "science of life" is a later appendage to the Atharva-Veda, and is also regarded as revealed knowledge. From these early beginnings the therapeutic system now called Ayurveda grew and continues to grow.

The first known medical school was at the University of Banaras about 500 BC where Susruta the Professor of Medicine composed his Samhita (Encyclopedia). Charaka a successor wrote another one seven hundred years later. These two Samhitas, the Susruta and the Charaka, form the basis of Ayurveda, which treats between 80% and 90% of the people of India today[196]. There does not seem to be reason to doubt that Ayurveda is the most ancient major therapeutic system in the world existent today and it is probable that all other existing systems are directly or indirectly derived from it, except in so far as herbalism derived from observing animals and rough surgery has always existed.

To the Chinese must go the credit of discovering acupuncture and pulse diagnosis. Itsing, a chinese traveller, writing between 671-695 AD comments — "In the healing art of acupuncture and moxa and the skill of feeling the pulse, China has never been superceded by any country of India"[167]. However the theoretic basis may well have been Ayurvedic in origin where some treatments involve heating certain points of the body, and there is a brief discussion of this in the section on Tibetan Therapy.

In China, as suggested by Stephan Palos[149], therapeutics like Topsy, just grew. Families discovered remedies for certain disorders, passed them on, and by sharing this information with those interested, who were probably also natural healers, an indigenous style of therapy developed. This would be about the stone age in China which is much later than the European one, say up to 2000 BC. At this time there is evidence of stone needles being used for Acupuncture. There is writing on bone about herbal remedies in the period 1000-600 BC, which was also the time when the Yin-Yang principles and the five elements, earth, air, fire, water and wood were introduced into therapeutic methods. Shortly after this about 26 AD *The Yellow Emperor's Classic of Internal Medicine* was collated, almost certainly being based on much earlier oral transmissions[210].

As Buddists spread east, first into China and then Japan the therapeutic system they brought with them mingled with the local Taoist and Shinto ideas, influencing each other and producing a special sort of Buddism called Ch'an in China and Zen in Japan. Both Schools also contributed to the first medical training school set up in China by Imperial decree early in the 7th century AD.

In Japan the development of the indigenous system of therapy was broadly similar to that of China allowing for local differences. Today however, in the Peoples' Republic of China with about 500,000 traditionally trained doctors and 70,000 western medically trained doctors, there is active co-operative research being conducted on the relationship of both systems, and the older methods are being assessed by the application of the scientific method. In Japan the trend seems to be more towards westernisation, and the traditional methods continue mainly among the dimishing peasantry and the Zen Buddist monasteries.

With this brief historical summary in mind it seems impossible to give a concise description of oriental medicine as a whole. Yet there are correspondencies and an underlying pattern. The nature of man ensures this, in spite of the fact that his mental activity driven by the Jack Principle, is incessantly divisive.

The approach will be first to look at Ayurveda as being the earlier codification, which influenced the Chinese and Japanese traditional systems from the 7th century on, then at the Japanese traditional system as more reliable information on this is available to the author than on the Chinese, and to describe Acupuncture separately in chapter 2 having shown where it fits into the Japanese system. A brief account of Tibetan therapy will be added.

This approach is not intended in any way to disparage the Chinese system from which the Japanese is probably derived, just as the Japanese script is Chinese in origin. One of the most perceptive definitions of good doctoring ever given comes from an aphorism found in many works on traditional Chinese medicine including *The Yellow Emperor's Classic of Internal Medicine* where it is said that the inferior doctor can only treat the illness he was unable to prevent, while the superior doctor helps people to avoid disease by educating them to harmonise themselves and cure the illness before it is manifested[210].

The position of Tibet, lying between India and China, its isolation and intense religiosity, has ensured that its therapeutic system is a mixture. No one knows whether the influence of the Indo-Aryan civilisation extended to Tibet when it flourished, but it is more likely that the tremendous influence of Buddhism as it spread North and East from

India in the 7th century AD ensured its main similarity to Indian therapies though there is a strong element of Chinese influence; for Tibet, before gaining and then losing its independence first to Britain and then the Chinese Peoples' Republic, was part of the Chinese Empire.

## AYURVEDA

Strictly speaking this section should not have been written because the barriers of language, space and time have prevented discussion with an Ayurvedic practitioner. Yet there are good reasons for making an attempt to describe Ayurveda, for as well as being the oldest in the world it may also be the origin of others, which if all were taken together, outnumber by many times both as regards practitioners and those treated, the other major system Allopathy.

Another good reason is that Ayurveda is undersold outside India. Almost all Indian doctors in the West are registered Medical Practitioners, who are so westernised that they seem ashamed of the main system of therapy of their native land. A few, when they have accepted that an enquirer is genuinely interested and will not hold it against them, do discuss Ayurveda rationally, and admit its effectiveness, though they have little idea of how it works. I know of only one registered medical practitioner, who also is a practising homoeopath who also has a knowledge of Ayurveda[173].

Furthermore the Ayurvedic System itself has slowly become more materialistic in consequence of the increasing tendency of man towards physicalness and intellection during the past three thousand years. Both this and the feeling of diffidence Indians have in trying to explain their seemingly inexplicable science and philosophy to western minds, have lead to the majority of books written by Indians in English being either disparaging or suppressive, towards the aspects of the subject that are paraphysical, especially those written before and soon after the British left India.

Recently however, Indian metaphysics and yoga have been increasingly accepted in the West and there has been a change in the tone of work available in English on Ayurveda, and this may well be due to a greater openmindedness in the west to things eastern which allows such books to find a market. As far as possible these more enlightened versions of Ayurveda have been followed in writing this section.

**Theory**

Just as Brahman the all, the absolute, has three aspects, Brahma the creator, Shiva the destroyer and Vishnu the preserver; so, on the level of the individual mind, there are three types of activity, Rajas, Tamas and Satva which correspond to the active creating energy, the passive destroying or resisting energy and the unifying preserving energy. Similarly at the physical level of the body there are Pitta, the active energy of heat, often called the element fire; the resisting energy Kapha, the element phlegm which is cold, earthy, and Vayu the element or quality air.

These three energies or processes operate on three levels modifying them. The levels are spiritual, mental and physical and the correspondencies are as set out below:—

|  | Active Creative Positive Energy | Passive Destructive Negative Energy | Unifying Preserving Neutral Energy | Called in India |
|---|---|---|---|---|
| Spiritual level | Brahma | Shiva | Vishnu | The Gods |

|  |  |  |  |  |
|---|---|---|---|---|
| Mental level | Rajas | Tamas | Satva | The Gunas |
| Physical level | Pitta | Kapha | Vayu | The Doshas |

At the physical level, when the harmonising balance of these forces is disturbed they become doshas, and being three are known as Tridoshas.

The human being and the universe are composed of five elements called Bhutas. *Ether* is all pervasive and equivalent to sound; *Air* is penetrative and light, gives pressure and is equivalent to touch; *Fire* is hot, gives colour and is equivalent to sight; *Water* is flowing, wet and is equivalent to taste; *Earth* is heavy, inert and is equivalent to smell.

In Western thinking Earth, Water, Fire and Air are called the Four Formative Forces (Steiner)[212], or the Four Humours (Greek); the Ether, the fifth component of both these systems being regarded as omnipresent. One is tempted to say also omnipotent since sound through resonance can control the manifestations of the other forces, and one recalls the phrase with which the gospel of John begins, as well as the fall of the walls of Jericho to the sound of trumpets, to consider how mantras work, and remember the section on Cymatics in chapter 9.

The human body is made up of seven constituents or tissues called Dhatus. These are modifications and mixtures of the five Bhutas. They are blood, flesh, fat, bone marrow and semen. The body functions properly so long as these Dhatus are in balance, and in health there is a constant fluctuation in the Dhatus' proportions.

Food after digestion is assimilated and feeds the seven Dhatus of the body, when this is done the residue is excreted.

However, if there is an excess or deficiency in the food, or if it is not balanced in the right proportion of the 3 energies, the Tridoshas are upset, and this disturbance affects the balance of the seven Dhatus so that disease occurs[197]. Though wrong food is a common cause of disturbance, physical activity, sleeping, sexual habits, the climate, emotional states, physical surroundings, age and sex of the subject all influence diseases. Charaka reduces these to three main groups; firstly 'the excessive, deficient and wrongful administration of sense objects; secondly the climatic characteristics of heat and cold; and thirdly the misuse of intelligence[116].

Susruta has a wider classification as follows:—

1   Physical diseases which can be:—
    a)   Hereditary from the mother,
                or the father.
    b)   Congenital through disturbances during pregnancy.
    c)   Through disorders of the Tridoshas as mentioned in the preceding paragraph.

2   Disturbances of the Physical Environment:—
    a)   Weapons
    b)   Other animals

3   Acts of God or Nature:—
    a)   Seasonal due to weather or planetary influences
    b)   Witchcraft or Divine Wrath
    c)   Natural such as hunger, thirst and old age.

This is a pretty comprehensive list of factors by Allopathic standards, the more so when one remembers it is about 2,500 years old[117]

## Diagnosis

Ayurveda does not try to diagnose a disease. It recognises every person as a unique being with his own constitution and environment, living at a certain time and tries to evaluate the resulting disturbance in terms of the nature of the disturbance, mainly in the Tridoshas but also in the Five Elements and Seven Dhatus, trying to discover which is excessively active or inactive. The Ayurvedic physician tries to treat the patient as a whole, aiming to find a "true" medicine — that is one which cures a particular patient completely and does not give rise to any side effects or other diseases[198].

The techniques of evaluation of the patient and his systems include a very detailed history that can embrace astrological assessment. The physical examination is most detailed and includes urine, faeces, sweat, sputum and voice. Pulse examination in the Chinese style has been recorded in the writings on Ayurvedic medicine during the last three hundred years[199] but the slant of the enquiry is towards determining which Tridosha is dominant or deficient rather than whether the Yin or Yang force is dominant. This is an advance made since the days of Itsing 1300 years ago.

In passing it is worth noting that in Ayurveda, Vaya is less disturbed than Pitta and Kapha respectively, the positive, creative and negative destructive energies so that they, (Pitta and Kapha) probably correspond to the Yang and Yin of the Far Eastern systems. The five elements of the latter correspond exactly to the Bhutas of Ayurveda. But there does not seem to be anything in the Far Eastern system equivalent to the seven body constituents (Dhatus). It would seem that Ayurveda embraces more variables than the Far Eastern system and is therefore, though more complex to use, likely to be the origin of the latter.

## Treatment

It is recognised that some conditions are progressive and inexorable, some are only palliable and some are curable. In treatment not only the therapist, the attendant and the medicine but also the patient play their parts. Charaka says, "Recollection, obedience to instructions, courage and ability to describe his ailments are considered necessary in a patient"[200].

Cleansing by diet, fasting, baths, applications to the skin, enemas, emetics and blood letting may be undertaken first on the principle that a dye will not take fast if the cloth it is applied to is dirty. Care is taken not to weaken the frail, and to tailor the treatment to the individual.

Next appropriate drugs are given to bring the individual into a state where the Tridoshas, Bhutas and Dhatus are harmoniously balanced. The pharmacopoeia after so many thousand years of continuous development is refined and enormous. There are also the Atharvic ceremonies, amulets and mantras, Yogic methods of healing using breathing, hand and mental techniques[155][156].

These forms of healing (see chapter 6 and the section on Far Eastern Therapy) may well be in the future the most profitable forms of therapy, since everyone can do them in their simpler aspects. But they do need a significant degree of dedication, as well as an ability to survive the negative energies released by them, so the role of a whole time healer is certainly not for everyone and this is discussed in chapter 14.

The drugs used are herbs, animal products such as honey, fats, and oils as well as minerals and metals. In the past six hundred years the use of mineral and metallic preparations in minute doses (see Homoeopathy, chapter 8) has greatly increased, and tended to supercede older remedies.

All drugs used to be prepared by the practitioner and are administered as powders, pills, decoctions, tinctures, jellies and oils. Refined metallic and mineral oxides and sulphides, and oxides of precious stones (see chapter 9, colour and gem therapy) are also used. Nowadays there is a tendency to use drugs manufactured by pharmacists and efforts are being made to bring out an Ayurvedic Pharmacopoeia[201].

So far attention has been concentrated on the general internal disorders, but Ayurveda also has divisions of surgery, obstetrics, gynaecology, paediatrics, eye, and ear, nose and throat diseases and psychology just like allopathic medicine, as well as dealing thoroughly with sexual disorders.

## Organisation

There is no governing body of Ayurveda in this country. It is the major system of therapy in India, where there are numerous schools and Universities where Ayurveda is taught.

## Comment

I have no personal or second hand experience of Ayurvedic treatment.

In the account of Ayurveda just given, the intention has been to let those who know about it speak. Their tendency has been to look at Ayurveda from a physical angle — possibly this is intentional because they realise this is the viewpoint of most western people. Yet it is quite clear that though some Ayurvedic drugs may work at the chemical level, they are aimed at the etheric body and probably also at the astral or emotional body (see chapter 4 for an introduction to this subject).

The considerations which lead to this conclusion are the descriptions given of the anatomy of the human body where the organisation of many siras (nadis) has to be strained to fit in with the structure of the physical body, there being too many tubes travelling from one organ to another in a way that does not occur in the physical body — so one has to conclude that a supraphysical body is being described. There is also some other evidence discussed in the section on Tibetan Therapy that supports this opinion.

It is important to stress that Ayurveda is not just a physical system of therapy like Allopathy. Its origin in Atharva-veda was regarded by the Hindus as sacred. It operates on all levels of man. It is a true science of Life and links up with the spiritual through yoga (see chapter 5).

Some of the other systems of therapy have connections with Ayurveda, notably Homoeopathy (chapter 8), Colour Therapy (chapter 9), and Radiesthesia (chapter 13). The Bhattacharyas using pendulum dowsing in a magnetic field have selected mixtures of homoeopathic remedies suitable for balancing disturbances of the Tridoshas, Five Elements and Seven Dhatus. They point out that special mixtures can be made for individuals, but indicate that the advantage of the mixtures they suggest are their safety, wide range of action in many disorders, cheapness and facility for use in large dispensaries where the press of patients renders normal practice impossible[16].

Of all the therapeutic systems discussed in chapters 2 — 13 from Acupuncture to Radiesthesia, Ayurveda seems to stand out with the Far Eastern Systems and Anthroposophical Therapy, from the rest. These are ways of life as well as being therapeutic systems. Of the three it seems that Anthroposophy is less of a system than the others, for while it is in no way ineffective, it is somewhat unmethodical because it is the product of answers to specific questions put to Rudolf Steiner by medical practitioners, rather than something he designed, and it borrows from Homoeopathy. The Far Eastern and Tibetan therapies were most probably derived from Ayurveda, though they have interesting and productive variations. Nevertheless it is to Ayurveda that one should turn if trying to evolve a World Therapeutic System. It has an elegant complex theoretical structure and a widely based therapeutic field. All that is good from other systems could be grafted on to it.

## FAR EASTERN THERAPY

### The Theory of Yin and Yang

What we call God, and those in the Far East the Eternal Unchanging Spirit or Tao, comes into manifestation by a division into three. At the level of this world of phenomena the analogues of their forces are represented by the expanding Yin and the contracting Yang and the uniting force Ch'i, or Ki, which is invisible, vibratory, fluid, and omnipresent. Yin and Yang represent polarity, and the reaction between polarity and vibration produces patterns. In this way form is established. The natural world of stones and chemicals is the residual portion of the phenomenal world which also contains life, mind and spirit. The sequence of events is energy, vibrations and polarity, waves and patterns, pre-atomic states, atoms, elements and other physio-chemical manifestations.

As well as the materialising process which is spiral in nature, there is also a similar spiritualising process of matter. So there are two continuously operating processes one a Yang contracting force, and the other a Yin or expanding force. The process operates at different speeds for each type of manifestation according to their nature. For minerals it is slow, for living beings much faster.

Man exists between these two spirals as a transforming agent. He is a model of the universe himself. He is the Kingdom of Heaven on a small scale, but he does not have the apparatus to perceive this. Each spiral comes from infinity and returns to infinity and consists of a taking in and a giving out. When the two are made into one during life then the Kingdom of Heaven is entered [203].

In Chinese and Japanese therapy it seems that emphasis is placed more upon the changes in Yin and Yang, but the system is still triadic. In Ayurveda the third element is taken more into account as being active in its own right and the inter-relationship of the three elements are involved in both causation and treatment of disease.


### The Theory of the Five Elements

The most perceptive account of the theory of the Chinese medicine is that of the Japanese Nyoite Sakurazawa, known in the West as George Ohsawa. The difficulties arise from the fact that in Chinese calligraphy a limited number of symbols have many different meanings, and usually those who can translate Chinese well do not have the necessary depth of knowledge of the technicalities of the subject. Ohsawa was an exception, he did not need to translate and many years spent in the U.S.A. and France had made him acquainted with our ways of thinking. Nevertheless, I suspect the clarity of Acupuncture and the Philosophy of the Far East must owe a lot to Bruce Gardiner, who edited his text [144].

The idea of the Five Elements arises out of the musical scale which in China is pentatonic and derived by omitting the semitone notes fa and ti from the scale do re me fa so la ti do. This fits in with the five and seven elements used in Ayurveda, and in Western music, the Law of Seven described by Gurdjieff[75] and Ouspensky[146], as well as Steiner's ideas of seven fold organisation (see chapter 4).

However, there are some internal inconsistencies in the presentation of the ideas expressed in Ohsawa's book, and a lack of correspondence between the Five Element system as described by Ohsawa, Wu Wei-P'ing[237], the Lawson-Woods[120], and others[44][138] and both Steiner's and Boehme's where they overlap. Probably the reason for this is semantic, but a full discussion is out of place here, being a matter for native experts who have spent a life time becoming masters of their particular systems.

Briefly the Five Elements — Wood, Fire, Earth, Metal and Water are forces with characters related to their descriptive names both physical and emotional. One form of relationship is that one engenders the other; earth is the residue of burning; metal is found in the earth; water condenses on metal, or possibly for metal one should understand mercury in the sense that mercury is used by Boehme[84], and mercury is a liquid; water is essential for plant growth and wood comes from plants; finally wood is a fuel for fire.

The other sort of relationship is one of overcoming or submitting. Fire overcomes metal by melting it; metal overcomes wood by cutting it; wood overcomes earth by covering it; and water overcomes fire by putting it out. Different organs, tissues, seasons of the year, times of the day, certain therapeutic agents, acupuncture points, senses, pulses, and the forces of Yin and Yang correspond to the Five Elements and inter-relate through the first cycle of becoming, called the Sheng Cycle, and the second cycle of contesting, called the Ko Cycle.

To someone who is utterly familiar with the principle of the Yin and Yang and the cycles of the Five Elements, there is no difficulty in giving a logical explanation of any phenomena encountered, both as regards causation and correction. The author was impressed by this ability in one teacher of Japanese Theory — Michio Kushi, at a seminar in June, 1975. One had to admit that the system was more logical and penetrating than allopathic medicine, and unlike the latter, also a way of life for it dealt with right eating as well as the therapeutic use of food and right living as well as meditation and hand healing.

## Diagnosis

Diagnosis is by listening to the patient's description of his complaints and elucidating their mode of onset and time relations by careful questioning. The season of the year and previous diet of the patient are also relevant as is the time and date of birth.

The organ affected may be determined by routine physical examination of a type similar to the Allopathic system, but the usual examination is much more extensive than that of Western medicine. Examination of both pulses of each wrist in 3 areas, making twelve in all, may take up to half an hour, and this may be repeated at special times of the day, and because there are about 60 diagnostic points on certain meridians (chapter 2 on Acupuncture); these if painful on pressure give information about which organ is giving trouble and which of the Five Elements is disturbed and in what way.

The proportions of the body, the stance, many features of the face (in particular the iris, eyeball and ears), the nails, growth of hair on the face and head, all contribute to the diagnosis and suggest a treatment.

There are several aspects to diagnosis; firstly to locate the disease and decide which organs are involved, and consequently along which meridian the flow of Ki is obstructed, and where and in what way the balance of Yin and Yang has been lost. Secondly there are 4 categories of disease consisting of two pairs of opposites — too much energy and too little energy, and hot diseases and cold diseases.

The category of the disease decides the basic approach, to stimulate or deplete, to warm or to cool the patient, and the location of the disease determines the technique of treatment. Finally, once the manifested disease has been cured, the initial disharmony should be corrected and the patient rebalanced as it were. This is where the Five Elements are used but the Master Wu Wei-P'ing says this knowledge is only taught verbally to those students whom the master believes worthy to receive it[237].

## Modes of Therapy

**Diet** — The macrobiotic diet, so called from Greek words meaning great life — is a way of life according to the order of the universe, that is something greater than man, the microcosm or little universe. It is not only to be used as a way of life, but also therapeutically to alter the balance of Yin and Yang, and in treating cancer as well as many other disorders including baldness, worm infestations, allergies and atheromatous heart disease.

Nutritionally the aim is to eat 70% whole meal grain, the remainder of the calories coming from vegetables including seaweed, fruit and a little meat though this should biologically be far from man, i.e. sea food rather than mammalian meat. This diet is low in sugar, and fat, but contains all the essential elements and vitamins. Though of course the items can't be got in a super market.

The food is always cooked, often lightly, on the grounds that firing renders food nutritious. Eating raw food enhances its therapeutic effect because the plant nature has not been broken down by heat. It should be recalled that Steiner made the same observations about cooked and uncooked food (chapter 4).

Food is used therapeutically to alter the Yin and Yang states in a patient, and so affects the balance of these forces and changes his whole being.

**Medicine** — about two thirds of the medicinal agents are herbal remedies, about a quarter are of animal origin and the remainder are minerals. They are used to regulate Yin and Yang but many, such as ephedrine for asthma, are also found in Western Allopathic Medicine.

**Surgery** — Operations of a more simple type than those used in Allopathic medicine are employed where appropriate for many of the same conditions are treated under anaesthesia induced by Acupuncture. Sometimes the operations were not all that simple; there are references in some early Chinese sources to a heart transplant[211]!

The principles of fracture treatment are different from those of the Allopathic system, which consists of early forceful re-allignment of the fracture using an anaesthetic and uninterrupted fixation of the fracture by immobilising the joints above and below it. The Eastern method is gentle and intermittent restoration of the position of the fracture and frequent adjustments of the splints, which leave the joints free above and below the fracture. Herbs are used to pad the splints to aid the reduction of the swelling and encourage regrowth of the bone, and herbal remedies are also given by mouth for the same purpose.

The whole 'for and against' of both methods is discussed by the Allopathic surgeon Joshua Horn who worked from

1954–1969 in China. He concludes that methods combining the advantages of both systems had far better results than from either system. There should be more of this open-minded co-operation between systems of therapy[90].

**Acupuncture and Moxa** — These are frequently used where appropriate, but are only part of a much greater whole — see chapter 2.

**Shiatsu and Do-in** — The first is oriental massage done by a masseuse, the second is self-applied. In Japanese Shiatsu literally means finger pressure, and Do-in, self stimulation. Both are essentially pressures on acupuncture points following the meridians, though certainly not only just by the fingers; deep massage, joint levering and joint springing techniques are also used as in osteopathy and chiropractic (chapter 5).

Both are thorough, systematic and somewhat disturbing the first time they are experienced, leaving one feeling rather as if one has played a game of rugby football or had a bout of wrestling, without fatigue and sore places, yet strangely detached and at peace.

Both adopt a method of orientating the subject with the universe, and clearly follow principles similar to those described previously in this chapter, in that on Acupuncture (2) and T'ai Chi (5). They are used prophylactically mainly but when therapeutically, in addition to balancing the Yin and Yang, an element of healing comes into Shiatsu.

**Palm Healing** — There are exact ways of generating healing force which comes most from the centres of the palms of the hands. Without giving details these involve eating predominantly Yang food, avoiding wearing metal, using cotton underclothes, posture, breathing, percussion of the hands, breathing on them and vibrating them with the voice. The healer's breathing is synchronised with that of the patient and the charged hands are moved over the body in passes directed by the meridians and the organ chosen for treatment, while holding the hand about 1-3 inches away from the body.

Palm Healing can either be done as a pair (of one healer and one patient) or in unison with a group, with each person maintaining contact with the others. Anyone can heal provided that the instructions to generate the healing force are carried out and the aim to heal held in the attention and directed upon the patient, or by all the members of the group upon themselves.

**Spiritual Healing** — Here spirit is used in the sense of the Universal spirit or Spirit of God — of which each of us partakes and of which we are manifestations. The healing process here aligns the patient's being with the Universal Spirit, which, like the universe, is organised on a spiral form with proportions ruled by a complex threefold and sevenfold relationship.

Thus it is different from hand healing which is a regulation of the Life force Ki through which the forces of Yin and Yang control the physical body. However, the harmonising of the individual will express its physical results through the mechanism mentioned in the preceding sentence.

This form of healing is what in the East is described as Secret Teaching. This does not mean that it is hidden from anybody, but that it is without value unless experienced. Therefore it is in a sense hidden from those who cannot experience it, and it follows that it may be beyond the reach of the experimental method when those using that method try to verify the indirect manifestations of the results of the Secret Teachings. Such results depend upon those involved in the experiments being able to have the experiences.

Nevertheless such experiences are possible for all human

beings. However being truly human involves having a consciousness which is simultaneously open to the physical world, the world of Life, (Nature, Plants and Animals) the suprasensual world and the spiritual world; and this is rare. Most people direct their attention only to the physical and Life worlds, so their possibilities are limited.

The methods employed consist of adopting certain simple postures, by breathing while directing the attention to the pathway taken by the force contained in the breath, and by sound using certain syllables and chants.

The process of healing in this way can proceed either by a single healer following the ritual and treating one or more patients who remain passive, or two people can treat each other simultaneously, or many people can do the ritual together and treat themselves as a group. Distant healing can be performed by any number of people by directing the attention to the person or persons to be treated.

## Organisation

I do not know of any practitioners trained in the system resident in Great Britain. Information can be obtained from the East West Centre, c/o S.H.C. 507 Caledonian Road, London N7.

Michio Kushi works in Boston U.S.A. The address of the East West Foundation there is 359 Boylston Street, Boston, Massachusetts, USA.

## Comment

I must admit to being very impressed by the seminar given by Michio Kushi in London in June 1975. Clearly this was an all embracing way of life of which the therapeutics were only a part, so this system must join Anthroposophical Therapy and Ayurveda as the three ways which seem to be the most desirable to study in order to guide our ideas for future developments.

On the practical side — for it is useless to speculate 'one must try the experiment' — I followed the Macrobiotic Diet for four months. Twenty-four pounds (10.9 Kg) of surplus weight vanished without hunger or a sense of deprivation. This was far more than I thought was possible. I felt lighter, livelier and more alert. There were some aches as the skeleton adjusted itself, and a craving for sweet things vanished. Performance uphills improved and I swam over a kilometer non stop which I had not felt able to do for forty years. Now I eat a modified macrobiotic diet in order not to make difficulties for others, but the new weight and vigour have been maintained.

I have learnt about one patient with a carcinomatosis who was considered inoperable, who was treated by Michio Kushi mainly by diet. The tumour has disappeared and she feels alright at present. This patient was under the care of an allopathically registered practitioner who attended the seminar.

Deviations from a macrobiotic diet, excessive sugar, fruit, milk products, and an excess of Yin in the diet are stated to produce atheroma. Atheroma is the major cause of death in middle age now. If the diet can also help cancer here may be a simple and cheap way of reducing the incidence of these two major killers — clearly a thorough trial is called for.

An unbiased account of oriental medicine is given by Joshua Horn, a surgeon in "Away with all pests"[90].

## TIBETAN THERAPY

It must again be confessed that it has not even been possible to get someone acquainted with Tibetan practice to vet this section. The material has been distilled from the books of Evans-Wentz[51], Lama Anagarika Govinda[69], Theodore Burang[28], and the Rechung Rinpoche Jampal Kunzang's translation of one Tibetan book on medicine and his short history of the subject[11]. Yet there is little to be said about the theory and practice that has not already been dealt with in the two preceding sections of this chapter, for Tibetan medicine as one would expect, is a mixture of Ayurvedic and Chinese practices. It is broadly speaking an old style of Ayurveda plus Acupuncture and pulse diagnosis.

The importance of Tibet lies in its isolation and spirituality. The lack of contact it has had with the West has allowed Tibetans to preserve an intensity of spiritual activity unrivalled anywhere else in the world, and until 1959, unaffected by outside influences. How can comment on the taking over of Tibet by the Chinese Peoples Republican Army be unbiased? The benefits to the common people of a liberation from feudalism are undoubted[91], yet the resulting loss of spirituality in Tibet will be the world's gain as the leaven of the ideas carried by those who left the country work in the parts where they now live. Everything changes, nothing is lost. Let there be hope that the Chinese people will also learn from the Tibetan people.

From Tibet comes clear evidence of the existence of the higher bodies of man, and also that these bodies may be influenced not only by mental activity, but that they can be influenced by physical treatments applied to the body with the aim of curing physical disease. A good starting point for getting a grasp of oriental medicine is Burang's book on the Tibetan art of healing.

Burang who worked for many years in Tibet, says:— "The second body, this subtle counterpart of the coarse body-husk, is said to be permeated by thousands of channels of varying density . . . the great majority of these channels are so arranged that their paths coincide with those of many blood vessels and nerve fibres, in that they follow the same course winding themselves around them. This could be the reason why so many Asian healing practitioners tend to designate blood vessels and nerves by the same terms"[29].

These views are backed up by Evans-Wentz in an introduction to a translation of a Tantric book of instruction on how to develop these paths. He says:— "This system invisible to all save those possessed of clairvoyant vision, is the psychic counterpart of the physical nervous system"[52]. Lama Anagarika Govinda says:— "The channels through which these psychic energies flow in the human body are called Nadi (Tibetan rtsa) and follow the fundamental structure of the body in a similar way to the nerve system, though they cannot be identified with it, as has often been wrongly maintained. All attempts at proving it have only shown that the experiences of yoga can neither be measured with the yardsticks of Natural science, physiology and dissecting anatomy, nor by those of experimental psychology"[70]. Sometimes proof can only be experiential[57].

The term Nadi (or its alternative Sira) is sanscrit; in Tibetan it is rtsa or tsa according to which method of transliteration is used. Lama Govinda thinks that misunderstandings arise through translating it either as "nerve", "artery" or "vein". The colours red, blue and yellow used to describe the nadis may not necessarily mean that they are arteries and veins, but refer to the colour of the psychic force they conduct. Perhaps the best equivalent to nadi in English is that used by the Lama on page 134 — "channel", an alternative would be to do as he says and leave it untranslated.

Now if the chapter on Psychology in Jampal Kunzang's translation is read and the plates are examined substituting "nadi" or "channel" for vein, it will be seen that what are being described are treatment points for moxa and blood letting and acupuncture, for the lines of the channels bear only a general correspondence to the various pathways of the physical body [112].

**Comments**

Those interested in seeing pictures of how the higher bodies of man appear to a clairvoyant should consult *Man Visible and Invisible* by C.W. Leadbeater [123] which has recently been republished. Dr. Shafica Karagulla working with clairvoyants has described similar experiences with sick people only a few years ago and her research continues [107]. Dr John Pierreakos, a psychiatrist working in New York, can see the human aura and uses its changes to help in his professional work. The group he works with is researching into ways of recording and measuring this light energy field [152].

It is hoped that the information given here, and elsewhere in this book will help to persuade people that man's physical body is kept in being by another, invisible but just as real, organisation, and that this has been recognised all over the world for thousands of years. Scientists should realise that the inability of their science to prove the existence of the "second" body implies, not that the phenomenon does not exist, nor that the experimental method is faulty, but that they themselves are deficient in vision.

CHAPTER 12

# Psychology

### Psychiatry, Psychotherapy, Hypnosis, Auto-suggestion, Autogenic Training, Christian Science, Meditation.

An interest in mental activity has existed from earliest times. It may not have been called psychology and its language may have been unscientific, but it was there alright. Dr Andrew Weil points out that from early childhood people seem to have an innate urge to change their usual state of consciousness[224]. Psychotherapy did not begin with Freud in the latter half of the nineteenth century. The painfully slow system of psychoanalysis he originated was new to his time and gave startling results. Great credit is due to him for his life-long struggle to establish it against considerable opposition in a materialistic age.

Paracelsus (1493-1541)[86][148] was clearly aware of psychological disorders. Carl Jung's researches into alchemy showed that the ancients knew a great deal about mental activity[104][105]. The various forms of Yoga, some of which involve purely psychological activity display a deep knowledge of the mind and are about 5,000 years old[234]. These ideas are more and more being incorporated into modern psychotherapy, and models of the mind.

## PSYCHIATRY

The majority of doctors who specialise in mental disorders,

call themselves psychiatrists and treat their patients with physical methods, drugs and electrical convulsive therapy, ECT, which consists of passing a brief direct electrical current through the brain producing an epileptic fit which is controlled by a short anaesthetic and a muscle relaxant. This is effective in depression but damages the memory. Sometimes an operation is used which severs some of the nerves connecting the frontal lobes to the rest of the brain. This is called prefrontal leucotomy. Its result is that the patient becomes quieter and more passive. Both the procedures sound repulsive, but judiciously used they can be very successful in keeping a breadwinner earning, and producing a tolerable family life.

Behaviour therapy is another form of treatment used by allopathic practitioners. This adopts the principle long known in animal training using a reward, or an unpleasant stimulus to condition behaviour. Thus an alcoholic may be deconditioned by being encouraged to sip his favourite tipple, receiving each time an electric shock strong enough to be unpleasant. A fearful person constructs a list of his fears and places them in order of severity. Starting with the least upsetting he is made to experience it again and again, being encouraged and rewarded, till whatever it was no longer disturbs him. This method sounds coercive and suppressive, but the mind is very adaptable and it is surprisingly successful in practice.

## PSYCHOTHERAPY

Psychotherapy proper is often undertaken by Psychiatrists, but only for a small portion of their time. It is not taught, except superficially in a few medical schools. It is regarded as a subject for post-graduate specialisation. Very few general practitioners undertake psychotherapy. It is time consuming and the excessive work imposed by the 3,000 patients per doctor, as well as a system of pay based on a capitation fee, does not encourage its use.

It is not necessary to have a medical qualification to practice psychotherapy, people can be trained in Freudian (psychoanalysis) or Jungian (analytic psychology) methods and then practice. Psychiatric social workers are trained to help with those patients psychiatrists do not have time to treat or who need a lot of assistance. Some people take a degree in psychology at university and find that they have a talent for psychotherapy later. Others develop through Yoga, meditation, or one of the esoteric schools — Sufi, Subud, Arcane School or Gurdjieff Group, and find they can help other people.

About 15 years ago a British psychotherapist estimated that there were probably at least 10 practising psychotherapists for every one who had any qualifications[97]. Today it might be as high as one in twenty or even thirty. Counselling, as it is now fashionable to call psychotherapy is a growth industry.

### Theory

The Jack Principle mentioned in chapter one ensures that any unpleasant incident is not passed into the part of the memory from which it is easily recalled. Nothing is actually forgotten, everything is registered in the mind, but anything which is not registered as important, to which we do not pay enough attention, or is harmful to our self esteem, is soon forgotten or suppressed. In this way the mind becomes divided into a conscious part and a subconscious part.

This subconscious part is just as active as the conscious part. It is as if we had inside or around us another person observing and reacting to life, yet not able to speak and act through our voice and body. The subconscious part of ourselves has habits, and often more disturbed tender places, because of the Jack

Principle and suppression, than the outer personality of which we are aware. When it reacts to a situation it releases emotion which passes into the field of consciousness and influences the current reactions of the outer personality, producing apparently unreasonable fears or anger — or another reaction which the conscious mind finds disturbing because it cannot explain its behaviour to itself.

The subconscious part in fact rules our lives. Because we cannot alter that which is not perceived by our consciousness — our behaviour is controlled by a set of habits, often those of an angry frightened child, which we do not know about. Its rule however will only continue so long as we remain in ignorance.

Psychotherapy is the process of being introduced to those parts of ourselves we do not know. Split into a small conscious, and a large disturbed subconscious we are disintegrated and out of control — when we know ourselves and are integrated we have more control. Then we see what our problems really consist of, and in the light of this the way out of them becomes clear. They still remain, but can either be avoided or are so reduced in intensity as to be a trivial burden.

This process is relative however. We are like fishes swimming in an ocean of life which passes through our gills continuously giving us of itself. There is always more to come, and as much behind. Our gills should be efficient, smooth flowing, extractors of energy, we should be willing and undisturbed acceptors of life.

## Practice

The older methods of psychotherapy consisted of the patient lying on a couch and reporting to the analyst all the thoughts that came into his mind. From this material the analyst could, by observing when the flow of thoughts checked, discover where the disturbed areas lay in the patient's subconscious, and by suggestions and questions gradually allow the patient to find them out for himself. This was a slow process which might take years, or even for ever, as new problems are always arising. Generally a more active method is used in practice whereby the therapist points out likely difficulties, and the patient sees how their suggestions fit in with his experience.

Other means of obtaining material from the subconscious mind is by dreams (Freud and Jung), drawing and painting (Jung), reactions to ink spots (Rorsach), and more recently by a guided day dream in which basic stimulating situations and symbols are fed to the patient who lets his mind respond to these, either visually or in the form of thoughts, while lying relaxed. The significance of the symbols and his reactions to them are then explained to the patient who usually does not know what they mean when he is digesting them. This method is part of a system called Psychosynthesis introduced by Assagioli. It gives rapid results in many cases as not only the conscious digestive process, but partaking in the guided daydream seems therapeutic[3,4].

Another form of psychotherapy is that called logotherapy — the logo being derived from Logos or meaning. Conceived by Victor Frankl, it starts from the position that there is always meaning in life — "Man should not ask what is the meaning of my life, but should realise that he himself is being questioned"[58]. Frankl introduced the method of treatment by paradoxical intention[59]. This produces rapid results if the patient is strongly enough motivated to carry it out resolutely. It is not unpleasant but some people are too lazy and changeable to carry out anything long enough for it to be successful, or prefer to retain their problem, and stop it as soon as it begins to work. Supposing one has an irrational fear of dying. Then try and die, see yourself lying dead and keep it up. It sounds funny, but it works. Gradually the fear goes.

Meditation and some eastern psychological exercises are increasingly being used in psychotherapy. An account of one of these, a Sufi and also Buddhist exercise, which the author first encountered while working with a Gurdjieff School Group, and adapted for use in psychotherapy, has been described elsewhere. It is an excellent way of learning insight and self observation [56].

## HYPNOSIS

Hypnosis was practised for healing purposes by the ancient Egyptians, Chaldeans and Druids. In Europe Dr Franz Mesmer redeveloped it, but as he attributed its effect to the power of animal magnetism which was difficult to demonstrate, he naturally failed to convince the scientific establishment of his time how it worked, even though it worked well in practice. The same applied to John Elliotson — 50 years later and several others after him. However, people persisted in hypnotising, curing the previously incurable and having operations done without anaesthetic, so it gradually became accepted.

There is still no really good explanation for the state of hypnotic trance some people readily pass into when relaxed and gazing fixedly at some object. The trance is induced more quickly if there is a voice telling the subject to relax and go to sleep. In this state people accept commands and can be instructed simply to get better from their illness, or disturbed behaviour. Alternatively psychotherapy can be speeded up by taking the subject back through their lives instructing them to remember disturbing incidents which they have "forgotten". These incidents can then be explained to them and integration of the experience brought about.

For any one hypnotist about a third of the people he tries to hypnotise go into a deep trance in which they will have no memory of what has happened. But every one who is not so anxious that he cannot relax can enter the hypnotic state though it may not be a deep trance. A person who does not go into a deep trance with one hypnotist will do so for another. People can learn to hypnotise themselves using a word, or idea as a symbol of command.

The hypnotic state is not meditation. It is more like being awake with the personality's sense of itself being held in obeyance. Meditation is a state of tranquil increased alertness. In meditation there is an increase in certain rhythms (alpha and theta) in the electrical current from the brain (electroencephalogram, EEG) which are present neither in the normal waking state nor in sleep[216][217]. In hypnotic trance the pattern of the EEG is that of the normal waking state, or of sleep if the subject is instructed to sleep[8]. Presumably if the subject knows how to meditate and is instructed to do so it will be that of meditation. However in meditation one is not receptive to the suggestions of another person, in the way one is when hypnotised.

It is now possible to estimate the level of hypnotic trance by measuring the resistance of the skin of the palm to an electric current[31]. When this has risen to 33% above his normal resting level a subject will "take" a post hypnotic suggestion, whichever way the state has been induced. This technique is admirable for telling the hypnotists when the right level of trance has been reached by eliminating states which resemble but are not, hypnotic trance, such as deliberate deception, self deception and sleep. In meditation increase in skin resistance occurs when the meditative state deepens, just as in hypnotic trance — so these states are related.

Hypnosis has some dangers — there is the apocryphal story of a patient who wished to be cured of a fear of crossing roads. In hypnotic trance it was suggested he would no longer have this fear. He duly lost it and was elated. However, shortly afterwards he was killed when crossing a road. It may be lethal to try and desensitise patients by making them experience unpleasant but important disturbing episodes in their lives, if for instance they are asthmatic. A blundering hypnotist may get a patient to dig out of their memory when they are in a trance more than they can consciously bear. Nevertheless in skillful, understanding hands hypnosis can be a quick, safe way of helping people. It should be used more, especially now that there are good methods of measuring levels of trance.

## AUTOSUGGESTION

It has been reasoned that provided the right state of acceptance was there, the force of suggestion was what made hypnosis work. The suggestion did not have to come from a hypnotist, but could come from a subject himself. This lead Coué to develop autosuggestion between 1880 and 1910. By 1920 the idea caught on, and the catch phrase "Every day in every way I get better and better" was heard everywhere. It was not a question of will power but of relaxing and accepting the advice. Coueism soon fell out of fashion, but may have a place in the future, now that an individual can measure his own state of receptivity on a skin-resistance meter.

## AUTOGENIC TRAINING

Autogenic therapy is so called because it is self (autos) generated (gennao). The principle is exactly the same as autosuggestion (Coueism), but the way of applying it is much more sophisticated. The mind uses relaxation of the physical body in quiet surroundings, to gain the co-operation of the instinct moving system (see chapter 5), and the rhythm system (heart and lungs). When the three systems are in harmony, and alert yet tranquil, they are responsive to suggestions, particularly positive ones. A great many practical formulae have been worked out for use in self programming for dealing with all common symptoms and life situations.

Autogenic therapy (AT) is used mainly in Germany, where it was developed by Dr J.H. Schulz (1884-1970). Almost all the literature on it is in German with the exception of a monumental text book by Dr Wolfgang Luthe[135] published in America, and a translation into English of a popular book by Dr Hannes Lindemann[130]. It is little used in this country, but from personal experience, and use on a few patients, I think some people prefer it as a form of psychotherapy to many of those mentioned before.

Lindemann who was the first person to cross the Atlantic single handed in a canvas canoe, programmed himself for this feat by two simple phrases, "I can do it" and "Keep going West".

The start of the procedure, and a useful test to see whether a person will use AT readily, is to lie or sit with the spine straight in a quiet room and say to oneself over and over "I am calm and relaxed, my right arm is getting heavy". When this is achieved start saying "My right arm is getting heavy and warm", use the left if one is left handed. When this is achieved the process is extended and a wider programming can begin. A person who genuinely experiences heaviness and warmness at a first session even to a slight degree will usually do well at it. There must be no compulsion, no feeling of "I am the master directing the situation" otherwise nothing will be achieved. Quick refreshing rest periods can be snatched. One can programme oneself to like unpleasant jobs and concentrate in noise and confusion. It is surprising how life's problems and irritations seem to resolve after AT. Psychosomatic and even physical disorders benefit also.

AT can be used to treat hypertension and induce relaxation in stressful situations thus helping to reduce the tendency to coronary disease[136]. It can stop asthma, hayfever, colds, some skin troubles, ulcer symptoms and help with arthritis. It is particularly good with emotional and psychosomatic problems — anxiety, aggressions, compulsive behaviour, sex problems and addictions[130].

If it is wished, when the necessary basic exercises are readily performed, symbols may be meditated upon as in psychosynthesis. In fact they are so similar that one wonders whether the two methods had a common origin, or one borrowed from the other. I think a person who was skilled in AT would very likely be more responsive when imaging in response to symbols, than in the rather more direct approach used in Psychosynthesis. Though in many instances people do well on the latter alone.

The impression is left that AT does better with those people who find imaging a little too fanciful, and prefer not to pry into themselves. Another way of putting this is to say that it suits other-determined extroverted people who prefer to deal with life's problems rather than indulge in looking into the states which cause them to have the problems, and, as said in chapter 1, that accounts for the majority of people. It should be used more, for it is easily learnt and the subject does it on his own.

## CHRISTIAN SCIENCE

Mary Baker Eddy considered that ill health was produced by a lack of concordance with the Divine. This is in accord with the oriental view, and so far few would disagree with her. However, she took the extreme view that disease was really an illusion, and that by ignoring it and removing the discordant conditions and beliefs, if not by oneself then with the aid of a Christian Science practitioner, the disease would resolve. This works well enough for some of the people for some of the time. But when pushed to extremes and taken as part of a dogma of religion, and therefore supposed to work for all of the people all of the time, it manifestly breaks down. Certainly the Christian Scientists I know are in the main healthier and less prone to be disabled by minor illnesses than ordinary folk, but they get major illnesses which do not respond to their method of treatment just like everyone else. There is a good discussion of the subject in *Fringe Medicine* by Brian Inglis[98].

Health and Disease are a pair of opposites. Strive for the one excessively, and the pull of the other exerts itself. To attain the one extreme is to pass into the other. Life on Earth consists of dealing with opposites, there is a constant necessity for choice. The Art of Living is to exist contentedly here and now while placing one's attention on that which is beyond the opposites. This is further discussed in the last chapter.

## MEDITATION

More and more people are meditating because they find it makes them calmer and more able to cope with life. Sitting relaxed and pondering on a problem, or holding a beautiful idea, or a flower (see chapter 4 on anthroposophy for the anatomical significance of flowers) in the mind's eye allows the subconscious to come to the surface, and the other parts of one's being to speak to one. Sometimes this comes in pictures, as words, as a feeling, sometimes as a thought. Occasionally if one goes very deep one has no sense impressions, one does not think, one brings back no memory — yet one is not asleep but refreshed.

In meditation the skin resistance is high and the EEG shows an alpha rhythm. At deeper levels theta rhythms appear and may become continuous. These are two of the physical parameters of the meditative state which can, by Biofeedback techniques (see chapter 10) be used to train people to meditate[71].

Oriental methods of meditation such as Yoga[234,51] and Zen[222,143,193], and the Chinese method described by Wilhelm[232], use postures and breathing techniques which have the same aim but vary with the part of the world in which they were developed. I have a little personal experience of the Zen method and like it.

A part of Yoga is Karma Yoga. This is meditation in daily life. When the actions of living are permeated with loving devotion and non-identification of the sense of I with the action, those actions become Yoga. Digging out a blocked drain can be Yoga. In this way living becomes meditation — every moment is intensely valuable, imbued with vitality. One is here now.

The Sufi's specialise in training people to live in this way. Though sedentary meditation is of great use, life must be lived. It is not possible in the Western World to sit on one's bottom and contemplate the infinite indefinitely, one would not survive for long, but to live in the meditative state, observing the personality in action with one's attention also directed towards what is higher than oneself, is an aim towards real life.

Gurdjieff[76,77] was trained in the Naqshbandi order of Sufis. His teaching which was best described by his pupil Ouspensky has been influential in opening minds in the West to the possibilities just mentioned. I had experience of his teaching for ten years, and pay tribute to its value and effectiveness. It changed my whole life.

Transcendental Meditation is a relative newcomer in the west. Some people feel that fee paying for tuition in meditation is repugnant, presumably either on the grounds that everything should come for free out of the taxes, forgetting that organisations must have income to survive; or they think that things of the spirit are as light as the air and they are not getting something solid for their money. It is a good system conscientiously taught, and I regard it as good value. After being initiated into the method I had one vision of a symbol which also made me alter my way of life. This book is a result of it, and another experience which I have not yet fully evaluated but which in the long term will be more important.

To sum up, meditation is an important and valuable human activity of a more fundamental nature than superficial adjustments of the personality through psychotherapy and psychiatry. But people are all different and each individual must discover what suits himself — as cockney barkers say "Yer pays yer money and yer taikes yer choice".

CHAPTER 13

# Radiesthesia including Radionics and Psionic "Medicine"

It is unreasonable to separate these two recent subdivisions of therapy based on the radiesthetic faculty.

The Radionic Association was founded in 1943, and the Psionic Medical Society in 1968. They differ in details of qualifications for membership and style of treatment, but their theoretical basis and origins are the same.

**Theory**

Water divining works at a distance and can be done from a map. Not only water can be located; metals, people and objects with which they have been in close contact can also be traced. In water divining if the twig is gripped hard it will turn inside its bark. The dowser cannot prevent its movement. This implies that force is not under the control of the dowser, he is just a mediator. Nevertheless some experienced users of the pendulum believe they work by subconsciously picking-up information about the situation they are investigating, and that this is transmitted to the voluntary muscles which twitch and compel the pendulum to move in a way which gives information according to a previously decided convention. For instance, a swing forwards and backwards may mean 'yes' and from side to side 'no'. Alternatively one may use a radial diagram divided into small arcs each with a predetermined significance. Instead of a radial diagram a dial and a pointer can be used and the correct setting determined by a sticky sensation as a rubber diaphragm is lightly stroked by a finger.

The western pioneer of the therapeutic and diagnostic applications in this field was an American, Dr Albert Abrams[168]. Working from about 1900, he thought that the force involved was electric and, since he could perform at a distance, that the transmission might be radio waves. Hence the coining of the term Radionics. His and several subsequent instruments had variable resistances wired in series. In the circuit was a metal plate under a thin rubber sheet. When the dials were correctly set a finger rubbing lightly over it gave the sticky sensation mentioned above, similar to that experienced when rubbing over an acupuncture point.

In this method we have the phenomenon of resonance which occurs when the dials are "in tune" with something. But that cannot be applicable to the use of a pendulum which will answer yes or no. However it might well explain the very strong response when a twig is tuned into water. There are further complications. Some modern instruments will do just as well with or without any wiring. This suggests that the setting of the dials may be just an indicator to direct or tune the mind of the operator, or that the energy being used does not need wires, but just a model or diagram for transmission.

Before drawing the threads of the somewhat baffling phenomenon of dowsing together it must be mentioned that in using the pendulum some operator's minds will receive the answer before the pendulum starts to move. Therefore, to obtain reliable results an operator must pose the question in writing or use a standard chart, and distract his consciousness, by thinking of something else and only note the pendulum's response when it has clearly established itself.

There are two possible theories to explain the radiesthetic phenomenon in the light of the above statement. Firstly, either there are fields of energy given off by the dowser and the object dowsed for, and their interaction affects the twig or pendulum directly; or the inter-reaction affects the mind of the operator whose fingers then twitch to give the right response if his attention is distracted. Secondly, there is a universal field of consciousness into which people can tune and obtain responses in the form of resonance phenomena by directing their thoughts. Speaking from personal experience as someone who can use the pendulum, both alternatives are correct. Some dowse the first, and others the second way, and yet others both ways.

Gravity, the earth's magnetic field and possibly other forces come into it. For instance some operators of the pendulum take no account of where and how they work. Some avoid dowsing over anything that might induce a magnetic field close to them, even to the extent of working over an antimagnetic rubber mat filled with randomly scattered iron filings. Others think that consistent results are only obtained over strong magnetic fields, but that certain phases of the moon prevent accurate results[17]. The elucidation of how Radiesthesia works offers a fascinating problem which has yet to be worked out. It should be thoroughly researched.

Abrams found that people who are ill give a reaction not found in health, and this can be recorded on the dials of a machine as a set of numbers. Being a doctor he thought in terms of the diseases and pathology he knew about. So he made a diagnosis by relating the pathology to the numbers or "rates" on the dials of his machine. Later he found he could apply correcting numbers which cured his patients.

who were attached by wires to the machine.

Ruth Drown, another American, a chiropractor, found that it was possible by putting a spot of the patient's blood into the circuit, to treat the patient at a distance. The patient's presence was not necessary for the whole process, a piece of him would do instead. A few hairs have since been found to be the best witness for the patient, for blood transfusions alter blood spots. Lists of rates and the diseases to which they correspond were built up through experience.

In England between 1918 and 1960 Dr Guyon Richards was the first to take up research on Radiesthesia[169]. He correlated various diseases with their homoeopathic and allopathic remedies, as well as with colour and the aura (chapter 9 – Cymatics). Others gradually followed Richards, of these the most active was George De la Warr, an engineer. He developed Abrams' and Drown's diagnostic and treatment machines as well as a camera. His work is still carried on by his widow at Oxford[40].

From these early ideas, which have always been organised on the allopathic method of history, examination, diagnosis of the disease in allopathic terms and then treatment, a divergence began. Dr George Lawrence had been attracted by the idea of employing the method of diagnosis in order to use homoeopathic remedies[166]. By radiesthetically controlled questions it could be verified whether these remedies were suitable for that patient. If not, a further search was made for alternatives. The Radionic society stuck to the older method and broadcast treatment, but later as Eastern ideas of the constitution of man spread to the West, David Tansley who is also a chiropractor, added Chakra diagnosis and treatment, and broadcast colour therapy to Radionic therapeutics[194][195].

Dr Michael Ash has researched on Radiesthesia, Healing and Acupuncture since the nineteen forties.*

In 1973 Malcolm Rae demonstrated an alternative way of preparing homoeopathic remedies by treating water with magnetically energised patterns (chapter 9 — Cymatics). Rae's remedies can either be swallowed like standard homoeopathic preparations, or broadcast. They are being used by Radionic, Psionic and some Homoeopathic practitioners[153].

### Governing Bodies

**The Radionic Association,** founded in 1943, Field House, Peaslake, Nr. Guildford, Surrey. Enquiries should be addressed to the Secretary. Qualified practising members only are elected by examination. Associates may be elected from anyone over 18 who is sincerely interested in Radionics. 460 members — 98 Practitioners.

**The Psionic Medical Society,** founded in 1968, Secretary Carl Upton, LDS Birm., Garden Cottage, Beacon Hill Park, Hindhead, Surrey. "Membership open to all qualified doctors and dentists." 150 members — 9 Practitioners.

### Comments

I have had personal experience of Psionic treatment with benefit and know of several people with similar experiences. My wife has also had radionic treatment with success. Several other people I know have had successful radionic treatment also.

---

*ASH, M., *Health, Radiation and Healing,* Darton, Longman & Todd, London, 1962.

My own feeling about Radionic and Psionic treatment is that their divergence is trivial and based on personalities. An unorthodox society based only on enlisting medically and dentally qualified practitioners will find recruitment slow for reasons given on the section of Homoeopathy – Comments.

Radionics has always seemed unnecessarily complicated. Allopathy has to work slowly through a process of history, examination, diagnosis and treatment. It is the only possible way an intellectual, physical system can proceed. But diagnoses are intellectual concepts which a system imposes upon unique sick individuals. All that is required is for the patient to be put in touch with the treatment he needs. This should be easy to do using Radionics, and make the method much quicker. It would be simple to provide an adequate check. What could be neater or more direct than allowing the patient, or his witness, to select his own treatment without the interference of the mind of the practitioner on his system?

CHAPTER 14

# Tactical Solutions

It is against the background outlined in chapter 1 that the future position of the 'non-medically registered' practitioners should be considered. Indeed one could ask should there be systems of therapy? A system is an organisation protecting a vested interest. It can be mechanically operated at an intellectual level by almost anybody. However, within all systems, and outside them, are people through whose agency healing occurs. This ability can be inborn, or come upon a person later in life.

Some healers appear to work psychokinetically on the body, others influence the mind of the sufferer. Since there is no obvious explanation in physical terms, the usual reaction is a blunt denial that healing of this sort can occur. When it is too well authenticated to be amenable to the blind eye response, or ridicule, it is said to be miraculous. It can be considered an act of God, and the scientific observer will breathe a sigh of relief — his system of belief can remain intact, for the matter is obviously outside his brief. On the other hand the religious find such an event an exciting justification for their beliefs, and call it spiritual healing, so their dogma can also remain intact.

In fact there are many forms of healing, but only rarely is it truly spiritual. It is not a requirement of healing that the sufferer should have a particular belief. In order to be healed however, it is necessary for the subject to be able to bear and accept the changes in his whole being that will follow the act of healing. If he cannot learn, accept and change the healing will fail, or he will relapse.

A worn out part in a badly balanced machine can be replaced, but it will soon wear out again. The machine will never run smoothly for long unless it is taken apart, balanced and rebuilt. That is how it is with healing. The balancers and rebuilders of human beings are rare. The ability to heal is precious. It must be cultivated, but not organised. Once it is organised there will be a drive from people of good intent to try and become healers, and the defects of organisation will follow. When enough people take the trouble to develop their BEING, sufficient healers will appear for the needs of the sick. There is no need for tools or systems, for *man is the instrument.*

If mankind were to develop its full potentiality at some future time, people would be able to heal themselves psychokinetically, either individually or by communal activity, though there would certainly be a need for some healers with specially developed powers. However, this will not happen in the immediate future, so in spite of this attractive possibility, apparent necessity drives us into an urgent consideration of the immediate future and this, in spite of its dangers, involves organisation.

The following proposals could lead to healing without destruction, and the acceptance of disease as a normal part of growth — a message to be understood — a call for action.

It is with reluctance that more organisation is suggested, but changes are desperately needed in the Medical system, which is founded on the concept that the basis of disease is physical; and being practically a state monopoly, suffers (like all similar systems) from the operation of the law of diminishing returns.

This means that ever increasing costs have to be incurred to achieve the same result. Being a system it allows only for diagnosis consistent with that system, i.e. those which are expressed in physical terms. This not only condemns the sick to suffer until their disorder is expressed physically by behaviour or physiological breakdown, but often, by correcting only the physical outlet for a disturbance arising elsewhere in the sick person's organisation, forces another breakdown.

In such circumstances the standard remedy is to diversify into other, as yet unexploited systems. These, when fully used will suffer from the same defects as Medicine. But that time is generations ahead and our Being may change, before they too come to the point of diminishing returns. It would be better if we could change ourselves first, but this is not practical at present.

Financially at least, the medical profession can be regarded as the tiny head of a brontosaurus whose body consists of the manufacturers and distributors of the medicine used for treatment. The massive body needs food, and helps the head to find it. By far the greater part of medical research is paid for by the pharmaceutical industry which only supports those lines of research which will be profitable to itself. Therefore it is from the pharmaceutical industry rather than the medical profession that the main opposition to change is likely to come. Especially as what was a growth industry is now becoming stagnant, and the cost of a new drug is rocketing upwards. The Drug manufacturers too are suffering from the effects of the law of diminishing returns[227].

Though the mind of the brontosaurus is conservative and slow, it does think. Non-medically registered practitioners are all busy in this country. They are increasing in numbers, and are supported by people who have already paid for their National Health Service. Doesn't this mean that their systems work? When it is realised that the non-medical systems are effective, then medical practitioners will soon find out that they are also cheap. For they use either natural therapeutic agents, or can make such agents from water by homoeopathic or radionic methods, or they can treat directly by radiation, even at a distance. Not only are they cheap, but easily mass produced and easily applied on a large scale.

Once enough medical practitioners make the above realisations, there are bound to be rapid changes. There is already public disenchantment with the present situation, which deprives tax payers in a supposedly free country of the right to have treatment of their choice on the National Health Service. If the Government cannot appreciate the situation, perhaps a private Member of Parliament might do so, and sponsor a bill to preserve the existence of the unregistered systems of healing.

To someone who assumes that nothing is real unless it can be touched, tasted, seen, heard, smelt or measured, only body processes which have the same characteristics seem valid; but there are octaves of radiations which most can neither see, hear nor measure. Some people see ghosts, some are clairoyant. Every few seconds a cosmic ray passes silently through our bodies. Our seemingly solid bodies are permeable. After seven years not a single molecule of our body is the same. We have been totally renewed.

On a molecular scale we are almost entirely composed of space. Once the Carbon, Hydrogen, Oxygen and Nitrogen in our bodies have been burnt, very little ash remains. Once life has left a body, it decomposes rapidly according to the laws of physics and chemistry. Every living being has a radiating field which varies constantly and is unique. This can be measured[30][209]. There is a life renewing field which keeps the body in being. This is the important factor to grasp. Perhaps the best model from which to start a change of medical, physio-chemical thinking, is that of water divining.

Everyone has heard of water divining. People can earn their living by it. It is easily measurable and extensively verified. Some people are sensitive to radiations of water at a distance. They can register this sensitivity mentally or physically by the response of a rod, or pendulum held in the hand. Not only water can be registered in this way. Other substances, and living beings also affect the dowser, who can find them from a map, by dowsing over it, or by question and answer. Not all dowsers have these abilities, but they can be learnt with practice. In fact many people can dowse, but do not know it. The physical basis of these phenomena is the inter-reaction of two or more extra sensory force fields, which affects the physical response of the dowser. The alternative systems of therapy influence the force fields which control and maintain the physical body, either by adjustments to the body itself, or to the radiations which influence its force field.

In an ideal society people would be more conscious and responsible for themselves than at present. There would be few accidents, and little psychosomatic breakdown. The inherited diseases and those inherent in the materials with which our bodies make themselves, especially those called the miasms by Hahnemann (chapter 9), would be looked after by Radiesthetic and Homoeopathic treatment mostly in childhood. The method of manipulation practised by Chiropractors and Osteopaths would also be used mainly during growth to prevent much of the potentially physical disease which occurs in adult life nowadays. There would be little need for elaborate and invasive diagnostic machinery. The bulk of the treatment would be by healers, who would need no tools. Some of this healing would be of the type now called miraculous — for example the instantaneous healing of a fracture, called the "high healing" of Huna (chapter 7). There would be no question of the state being responsible for running a gigantic service to treat the diseases of its citizens. They would be ready, and able, to be responsible for themselves.

This ideal future would take some generations to realise. An intermediate state would come about by the gradual realisation of the benefit coming from the increasing use of ways of healing which deal with the pre-physical states of disease. There would be more prophylactic use of Radionics, Homoeopathy, Acupuncture, Osteopathy, Chiropractic and Psychotherapy. These would put less demand on the hospitals and reduce the cost of expensive physical treatment. The dominant position of Allopathy would be replaced by the use of each method in its appropriate field of disease. There would be emphasis on being healthy rather than mere correction of breakdowns of health. The resulting diversification of methods of treatment would prevent the diminishing returns situation. The centres of excellence would move outside the hospitals. The sort of organisation which would assist this development would be a single registerable qualification of health and healing, in a real *Health* Service.

This would entail changing the General Medical Council (GMC) into a General Health Council (GHC) to govern all the systems of healing on an equal footing, and lead ultimately to a common training for all the systems ending in the single qualification of Registered Health Practitioner (RHP). Probably the number of systems any one individual could practice should be limited to about three. The selection of students for training should emphasise ability and dedication, not just early academic scientific capacity. Nurses and medical technicians of experience should be welcomed, and no one accepted direct from a school or university without a year working in a hospital or the ambulance service.

Healing is in a special category, and the best way of protecting the public would be for those genuine healers who wished for the protection and recognition afforded by a qualification, to apply for an honorary qualification of RHP (healing), which would be awarded at the discretion of the GHC. A true healer does not need to pass an examination. Healing is not something that can be learnt intellectually, taking a course of instruction like medicine.

King Henry VIII recognised the profession of Herbalism in 1542 by signing an Act of Parliament to protect them from persecution by the Company of Physicians and Chirurgeons, but also to curb the activities of the wise women, witches and itinerant pedlars of herbal remedies. The Medicine Act of 1968 made provision for the supply of herbal remedies by a consultant herbalist on his own responsibility. It is therefore an acknowledgement of the first step made by Henry VIII towards a future where the many disciplines of therapy practise alongside each other.

In England Homoeopathic remedies can be prescribed by Registered Medical Practitioners on the NHS. Other steps have already occurred in the U.S.A. by the incorporation of Osteopaths and Allopaths and the registration of Chiropractors; in Germany by the Heilpraktiker qualification, in India where many systems are registerable[174], and in China where the old methods of treatment, of which Acupuncture is only a part, operate alongside Western Medicine. There is also in existence the International Federation of Practitioners of Natural Therapeutics. In this country there is the British Committee for Natural Therapeutics and the Paramedical Practitioners Committee for Natural Therapeutics. These titles are a mouthful of words and neither Acupuncture nor Radiesthesia is strictly natural. Surely General Health Council would come more easily off the tongue and express its aims, as well as being a more suitable title for a Governing Body wishing to co-operate with the existing organisation? It would be well worth considering a change of title. The controlling associations and colleges of non-medical systems of treatment, might be more active in supporting a transformed and renamed council which would represent them all.

There are too many small societies representing practically the same interest. Splinter groups are a tribute to independence of mind, but are politically weak. For example there are Radionics and Psionic "Medicine". The latter group insist on prior medical qualification, but many radionic practitioners use psionic ideas and methods, and the restricting effect of insisting on a prior medical qualification has kept homoeopathy in an numerically weak state, as well as delaying its evolution.

The latter's methods of treatment have been adopted by Psionic practitioners, who also manufacture therapeutic agents from standard homoeopathic remedies, and use them either by mouth or radionic transmission.

It is clear that a lack of unity has lead to confusion. To an outside observer, even a favourably disposed one, there seems to be practically no difference between Osteopathy and Chiropractic, except in their names. That difference is due to the phenomenon of the simultaneous occurrence of the same idea to several people in different parts of the world, once a certain need arises. Nevertheless there are encouraging signs that efforts to co-operate are being made in the unregistered systems of treatment. There is a mutual tolerance and exchange of ideas at a personal level, between the practitioners of the different disciplines.

Once the non-registered practitioners have formed a strong General Health Council to represent their interests, it should form registers of existing practitioners and organise the formation of a college to teach new recruits on the lines already mentioned. In several disciplines this has already been done. Until this can come into being, the associations at present governing the various disciplines should train, or vet new applicants, and submit them to the GHC for registration. The GHC would then publish a list of Registered Health Practitioners indicating the specialities and qualifications.

This would protect the public.

At about the same time that the GHC is formed it would be a good idea if a College of Health Practitioners could be set up in London with outpatient facilities, a research department, library, teaching school, committee rooms, and if required, offices for those affiliated associations which need them. Some of the funding for this operation might come from the business community, whose company directors worry themselves to an early death under medical treatment, having about a seven times greater chance of dying before 64 than the average man[158]. In return the college would be able to offer advanced health screening and early treatment services by co-ordinating several of their methods. It would not be difficult, if the co-operation of the Medical Practitioners was available, to do a prospective trial of this service against that at present run for the Institute of Directors by their medical service. If planned carefully this trial would yield much useful information on the possibilities of the unregistered systems, and the type of disorders which they are best able to handle. They may have considerable possibilities in the emergency fields, and not only in mild chronic, variable, self limiting disorders as some observers imagine.

In general the unregistered practitioners in this country often refrain from treating conditions that can be serious and need hospital admission, because they do not want to risk trouble, since they do not have a licence which protects them from prosecution except for professional negligence. In fact many of them do treat their patients, but advise hospital admission as well under a medical practitioner, who often does not know what is going on, and wonders why his patient got better so miraculously.

There are encouraging signs for the non-allopathic practitioner. In this country some small hospitals are developing. One is the Ramana Health Centre, dealing mainly in homoeopathic treatment. Another sign is the recent co-option of the International Federation of Practitioners of Natural Therapeutics on to the liaison committee of the E.E.C., whose function it is to advise on how the laws of the community relate to the functioning of all the liberal professions. These laws are due to be harmonised by 1978. The World Council of Churches has initiated unconventional ways of health care in Korea and Rhodesia. In Brazil, Italy and the USA there are small ventures where medical and unorthodox practitioners and healers co-operate.

Certainly such changes are against the present policy of the General Medical Council, though there is a growing tendency among medical practitioners to suggest to some of their patients that they might do better to consult a practitioner of another discipline. The change that the medical profession could make would be to be more tolerant, open minded and less inclined to intellectual hubris.

A position is only vulnerable when those in it feel it must be retained. Nothing in the Universe is static. Everything is constantly changing. To stand still is to start to die. Occasionally to stand still will result in immediate death; one may have to run like hell to survive, or one may even have to admit that black is white. To survive is to be able to come again another day. Living rightly consists in adapting to life all the time. Giving to each moment what is appropriate to it. This is a state of constant evolution. A welcome recognition and helpful co-operation should be given to all colleagues dedicated to the assistance of others.

It is time for medical practitioners to realise that they must diversify their monolithic system, especially as it seems it will become more than ever before a state monopoly, if the present Government enforces its expressed intentions. If this happens, and no diversification of methods of treatment occurs to offset the operation of the law of diminishing returns, the people of this country will have a growing millstone of cost and disease round its neck which will drag it steadily down.

In these circumstances independent, alternative systems of treatment will flourish, unless they have been hamstrung by legislation. Theirs is indeed a difficult choice, either to seek the protection of legislation, and risk being sucked into the maw of a monolithic National Health Service, or to lie low, and profit from public disenchantment with the National Health Service at the risk of being outlawed. But at least the alternative systems have a choice. The Allopathic medical system does not. It must diversify or price itself out of credence.

Many European countries prohibit the practice of the unregistered systems of treatment. In 1978 the laws of the members of the EEC are due to be brought into line with each other — so time is short. This situation provides an unusual opportunity for creative co-operation. Medicine needs to diversify. The unregistered systems need to preserve their legal existence. They also need to have their theory and fields of activity carefully investigated to determine what each does best, for it is not a question of abandoning the scientific method, but widening its fields of application.

A method is not the system it has engendered. The nature of the latter is determined by the outlook of its operators. That outlook does need to change. Surely the suggested union of scientific medicine with all the other ways of healing would be a fruitful relationship for the future of our health care.

CHAPTER   15

# The Strategy of Life

**The Problem of Choice**

When mankind was young there was co-operation with Nature. The fall of Man could be said to start from the time the Jack Principle began to operate. From then on Man chose not to co-operate with Nature — his environment. The ability to choose separates man from the other living beings on this planet. Choice introduces the concept of opposite alternatives, of polarity. Animals and plants have little choice. They are ruled by their surroundings and needs, so that they conform willy nilly to Nature's laws.

Man, with the power of choice conferred on him by his possession of a strong ego development, can go against Nature. This is his usual way of going beyond his own natural self. He ignores the fact that everything is a food for something else in the dynamic hierachy of Nature. He may know that plants capture minerals, water and sunlight to turn them into food for animals by photosynthesis; that from then on larger animals feed on smaller animals and Man eats all. He does not ask what he is food for, what is his purpose, what should be his aim.

Most people see Man just as a superior animal and act accordingly. The ability to chose leads him to think in terms of opposites, so he assumes himself to be the ruler of Nature and adopts an unco-operative attitude. He tries to bend her to his will, modify her and even be downright anti-Nature. This is his way of going beyond or transcending Nature. He feels the urge to explore; he plans to go into space; he burns up the earth not considering the consequences of the mess his activities create. He just thinks so long as I'm alright Jack, and makes changes without any other aims. The result is restless conflicting activity from each individual or group.

Actually he is here on earth to co-operate with Nature and to learn that what he must transcend is himself. It is only when he can transcend his ego that he can be food for what is higher than himself. If he cannot do this he remains part of the animal energy cycle.


**The Conditions for Doing — Aim, Consciousness and Will**

No one can do anything — unless firstly he has an aim or intention; unless secondly he can sustain awareness of that aim against the constant distractions of his own mind, the demands of his body and his environment; and thirdly he must value that aim sufficiently to make the efforts needed to carry it out. He must really want to achieve that aim. If these three conditions are not met, there can be no result from all his activity — merely a reshuffle of possibilities — only endless change.

First there must be *Aim* (intention, formulation, thought and faith); *Consciousness* (attention, energy and hope); and *Will* (valuation, care and feeling). The use of so many words for the same thing makes for difficult reading — the prose does not flow well, but please be forbearing and look at the meaning behind the words. Communication through words is difficult, once crystalised in words an idea immediately loses some of its meaning. When these words have been through another mind the meaning has undergone further change, just as my original idea changed when I expressed it first in my words. For instance some people would call the whole of this process thought, others would call it will, others mental activity.

The moment we hold our attention steady to formulate any concept we cease to be aware of the present and have moved either into the past, or by use of imagination into an assumed future. Our minds are never conscious in the now, only in the static past and a fantastic future and this is only a projected kaleidoscopic picture of our past ideas and so inevitably false. This is the dreadful prison to which our minds and personalities confine us.

The terminology used above is not my discovery, but it has been confirmed for myself as truth by years of self observation as well as the study of other's minds and by their observations of their own minds. It has been confirmed by practical experience[54]. Its source for me was Sufic, (or was it Tantric?) via the teaching of Gurdjieff[73][147], and also the New Testament[151]. This basic triadic form is also found in prechristian religious writings, Hindu and Buddist, as well as in Steiner's thought.


## The Importance of Aim

Our approach to health is a special example of our general attitude to life, so let us consider first how we regard our lives. That we value life is certain — we struggle hard to stay alive in dangerous circumstances — to feel one is going to die is for most people a fearful experience, and suicide is universally accepted as abnormal. That we are conscious of being alive is also an equally acceptable truth. It is only in our life aims that there are wide differences.

A peasant living in an area liable to drought will make his

life's aim survival by growing enough food to live, and if he cannot cultivate land he will look for work that will earn him enough money to eat. If he cannot work he will beg, or overthrow his government if it is weak enough. In an affluent society he may seek money, power or love rather than survival. His horizon for aims widens and the more complex his society the more possibilities he has. He may even realise that life is an endless process of becoming, that as soon as he attains one aim the satisfaction of achievement disappears. Then he turns to another, which, when achieved also proves unsatisfying. So he may ask himself what should be his real aim. Why am I here? Where am I going?

**Disturbances of Aim**

He will find that there are many people who are only too glad to tell him. There are the evangelists of every creed, sect and philosophy, just waiting for such innocent fodder. One can recognise them by their intolerance of any aims other than their own, their certainty and violence when their beliefs are shaken.

It is among the disturbances of aims based on the emotion Faith, which gives direction to mental activity, that the main difficulties of mankind lie. The disturbances of Hope and Charity (care and love) lead mostly to individual suffering. Disturbances of Faith are important because they lead to feelings of excessive certainty (self righteousness) and excessive uncertainty (fear). They manifest as a desire for order or disorder; to do good or do evil. These are fruitful fields for the operation of the Jack Principle. All the socially acceptable abuses of humanity such as wars and exploitation of the poor and gentle, come from the disturbances of faith. This does not mean to say that Hope and Charity are not important. They are, but do not primarily cause the difficulties, because people recognise their negative aspects as unpleasant feelings.

The disturbances of Faith, even fear, are not so easily recognised as negative.

The theory and practical manifestation in the personality of the negative disturbed emotions have been worked out elsewhere[55]. It is not necessary to labour the importance of aim further, and after this short digression it is time to turn back to the development of the individual's reaction to life and his question, "Where am I going?"

## Small and Great Aims

He is now in a position to see that there are two sorts of aims. One is to do with position in Society — in life, and another sort of aim that has to do with something beyond life itself — with something far greater than himself. Also there are small variable aims which change according to circumstances and big aims that vary according to the type of person one is and with ideas one has encountered but not according to circumstances; they are outside life.

Sometimes a person has a feeling of searching or inner disatisfaction with life aims and is attracted by the great aim — but many grow to find this through experiencing the inadequacy of small aims to satisfy. Others, certainly the majority, are so taken up with the action of the Jack Principle in the field of Negative Faith that they spend their lives busy in the pursuit of their small aims and are satisfied.

## Tactics and Strategy

Small aims are the tactics — large aims the strategy of life. Now it is possible to have good tactics and still lose a war, but it practically never happens the other way about. Wilhelm Reich pointed out that tactics "lead one only to a premature grave"[164]. The implication is that strategy has to do with eternal life — but this theme will be taken up later. It is necessary now to consider these ideas on aim, as applied to life and its meaning, to Health and Disease and their meaning and relationship.

## Health and Disease

There is a saying — "There are many diseases but only one state of health". This is not true. Each one of us is an unique individual and each one of us goes wrong in an unique way. The systems of therapy that give a standard treatment of a specific disease are imposing themselves on the individual and are bound to give poor long term results, though of course they will be more statistically predictable than those systems which consider the individual first. "There are as many states of health as there are human beings"[191].

If a thorough investigation is made everybody will be found to have some physical defect as well as an emotional problem; we are all neurotic and imperfect. After the age of 50 every man has atheromatous disease of his heart's arteries and by the age of 60 women have caught them up[142]. Also after 50 it is usual to have more than one physical disease present in our bodies. In fact we may well have three of four. But the facts do not mean an individual may not feel and be healthy even though his body is not perfect.

Inside our make up is a psychological growing point — an urge to evolve, to create, for each of us it is that unique individuality which makes us different from each other. This has to contend with the Jack Principle of the personality and also with external influences of life and the universe. If it gets swamped we feel frustrated and do not digest the impressions taken in during daily life and we become ill, (just like wild animals — who are much more healthy free than when they are caged), tensions and frustrations build up; noise, crowding and stress take their toll, because we are not expressing our lives as we should. This state produces the diseases of stagnation which can be emotional, such as "Don't want to know", "Don't care", depression and hysteria, or physical such as obesity and atheroma.

The other side of this pair of opposites is trying to digest impressions excessively, to enquire "Why?" excessively. This leads to fussiness, hair splitting and worry, and over involvement in everything and this produces the diseases of over activity — for example hypochondriasis, anxiety states, hypertension and excessive thyroid activity.

Difficulties arise because people identify themselves with their physical bodies — so that they suppose that if the body is abnormal they are unhealthy. Now this leads the fussy excessive digester who has an itch to be perfect, straight to his therapist. A therapist, whatever system he practices, has an itch to put things right. Each fulfils the other's need.

## The Nature of Disease

There is no simplistic cause of disease. It exists because nothing is perfect on earth, there is an element of error — a limitation — because everything has a lifetime. The only certainty is death — yet life is eternal, everchanging. Since death comes about through disease the existence of disease must be accepted as normal.

Everything in the universe is related to everything else. "Every entity large and small is therefore continually being qualified and modified by, and is continually being adapted to, the never ending succession of stresses and strains, major and minor, transmitted through the web of cosmic structure as nature strives to maintain a state of dynamic balance. That which we call disease is therefore a temporary localised unbalance, a bit too much of something, or not quite enough of something else, too much pull from one direction and not enough from the other"[231].

## The Psychological Component

Nearly every illness in a previously healthy person is preceded by an emotional disturbance[48][45], the giving up — given up situation; but disease is not only caused by mental disturbance, there is always a structural component. Disease produces mental disturbance; there is a play back, a disturbed body stresses the mind and disturbs it. Enduring pain is depressing, and the fear of death in a person who has never assimilated the idea that he will die can be terrifying.

So, while it is true that 70% – 80% of people who seek advice from the therapists, do so because they are emotionally disturbed and have some slight disturbance of their body functions or even severe ones due to their emotional trouble, probably the best formulation is to say that there is a psychological component of every illness, and that on the average 50% of ill health is physical and 50% mental.

It has been illuminating to study other methods of therapy and find that many disorders have a simple physical basis that can be easily put right by, say manipulation or a short course of homoeopathic treatment, and yet had that patient remained under allopathic treatment and gone on complaining and suffering, getting depressed and anxious, finally even rude and pressing, nothing would have been found wrong with him and he would probably have been referred to a psychiatrist, since one of the ways mental disorders are diagnosed is the presence of emotional disturbance without discernible physical cause.

The idea that disease is about half emotionally induced and half physical is not new. The oldest statement of it known to me occurs in the Mahabharata variously estimated to be from three to five thousand years old. "There are two classes of disease — bodily and mental. Each arises from the other. Neither is perceived to exist without the other. Of a truth mental disorders arise from physical ones and likewise the physical disorders arise from mental ones"[202].

**The Factors of Disease**

There are four main factors to consider in any disease:—

*Passing Time* imposes limitation of direction — an individual life begins and grows fast. Time moves slowly for the child. As the life continues time moves faster, and physical decay sets in to end finally in death. The individual's consciousness of time alters his ability to digest impressions from his every day life. Adverse undigested mental impressions remain in the individual and produce the stress of life. The modern environment is full of more adverse impressions than it used to be. One only has to live in the country and go to a town in order to appreciate this fact. The death rate in stable remote country areas without other adverse environmental factors is lower than that of towns — so is the average blood pressure level. To sum up — Time controls growth and decay; and the ability to assimilate impressions, which is related to consciousness of time, reduces stress.

The word *Environment* describes the external influences which affect each individual. Personal relationships in the family are the earliest and most important, though the astrologers would say otherwise, and there is evidence that there is a correlation between birth time or conception time and subsequent careers which has already been mentioned. My personal view is that there is a lot in Astrology — not the simple sun sign stuff of the daily press and most magazines, but a careful individual assessment by a competent operator will reveal possibly unrecognised tendencies in a person's make up, and indicate times when conditions are adverse or personal failings may occur. This knowledge is useful to anyone who takes an interest in managing his life. For example the use of a book on astrology which gives the influence of the 28 phases of the moon upon a person's sun sign will often give a revealing understanding of certain psychological problems which otherwise defy explanation and this can be used to advise people how to help themselves. I use this from time to time[150].

Social conditions affect people profoundly — to elaborate this fully would take another book. To give a few examples: efficient sewage disposal and plenty of pure tap water vastly reduce death from infectious diseases; maternal deprivation produces a high incidence of children subject to clashes with the law, poor interpersonal relations, nervous breakdown and suicide; the criteria of insanity vary greatly in different parts of the world; Child and wife battering are in the news now, these have devastating immediate effects and it will only take a few years for their long term effects to be evaluated.

The operation of the Jack Principle has probably the greatest affect of any single factor, as it conditions the whole pattern and behaviour of the social structure as well as that of the individual.

Diet is partially varied by the structure of society and partially by the geographical situation. A rich industrial society can afford to let its home grown food production fall and live off the produce of poorer less industrial areas. This leads to famines, because the poorer areas try to buy the manufactures of industrial ones, for food which just grows with care and attention is cheap while the manufactured products need the application of energy produced by the breakdown of a previously existing state of energy and this is expensive, not only in its immediate use but in its accumulative long term effects and waste product disposal. The poor agricultural areas have to sell so much of their produce to get the manufactured goods, that they have no reserves for bad years and in large parts of the world little enough in good ones.

Poor quality eating produces illness either through many types of deficiencies which are common even in wealthy well organised societies, but naturally are practically universal in famine areas, or through excesses. Obesity is, like atheroma (fatty degeneration of the arteries), a slow plague of man and the two are associated. In Europe and the USA atheroma is now a major killer.

Narcotics, in which are included smoking and alcohol should be mentioned here. When taken in excess they produce disease — though many of the newer narcotics seem to carry a far smaller death rate than the fiscally accepted, old faithfuls, smoking and alcohol.

The ingestion of chemical compounds as contaminants of foods, "permitted additives", medicine with "side effects" and industrial by-products, all produce diseases and form part of the environment.

Varying climates induce different illnesses, mainly those transmitted through the different sorts of parasites and animal carriers of diseases that affect man. Though extremes of temperature also produce certain disorders such as heat stroke, cold coma and frost bite.

Radiations such as sun spots not only influence the weather, but also seem to be associated with physical and mental disturbances; so do the phases of the moon. Magnetic fields, x-rays, sound and possibly other forms of radiation, as yet not appreciated, can also influence living organisms, adversely.

*Inheritance* can be both physical and Karmic. Physical inheritance is simple to understand. Its basis is in the chemical messages coded in the nucleic acid spirals that form the chromosomes and these are passed from one cell to another as they divide. Many tendencies to various forms of breakdown are transmitted by such physical inheritance, some are truly familial and others are acquired from environmental factors such as maternal illnesses and defects of the chemical components of the molecules of the nucleic acids.

Karma is harder to understand. It is the idea that unfinished business, tendencies and psychic debts may be brought from one life to another by a soul in successive incarnations. Some Karma manifests itself as physical illness, others as a life situation; the theory being that a soul chooses a body complementing its need. Karma can be regarded as destiny or fate.

The idea that a conscious element (the soul) passes from one physical life to another is widely held in the East. In the West, where Christianity has dominated thought on such matters, it was only abandoned in AD 551 by the Council of Constantinople when belief in reincarnation was declared a heresy.

In spite of the re-editing of the scriptures which must have followed, a number of references to re-incarnation remain (Matt. 11.14, 16.14, 17.10-12; Mark 6.14-16, 8.27-28; Luke 9.7-8, 9.18-19, 11.24-26, 19.9; John 1.19-22, 1.25-26; Paul 1 Cor. 15.45; James 3.6; Rev. 3.12; Psalm 90.3). A useful account of the subject was given by Rudolf Steiner in the Manifestations of Karma[192].

It has already been pointed out that each illness contains a message that some error or disharmony in one's life needs correction, but when the origin is Karmic it is certainly not due to the environment, time nor the response of the individual ego to these two factors. Karmic influences can only be changed by conscious psychological suffering and otherwise cannot be avoided.

Therefore a certain amount of disease and suffering is inescapable. Perhaps a third of all illness is of Karmic origin. One of the signs by which it can be recognised is when in the course of a disease the patient responds far less well than usual to treatment which is usually effective, or gets a series of relapses and complications which is out of the ordinary. To go on doggedly enforcing treatment may well cause that patient to suffer unduly by prolonging their life. It is a difficult decision for a therapist to take and he would be helped if the services of people with trained intuitive faculties were available for consultation in such matters. This idea should be developed in the future.

Finally the *Unique Individual's reaction* to these three external factors *Time, Environment* and *Inheritance* determine the type of disease he suffers whether mental or physical. This reaction should be regarded as a process of becoming. A unique individual consciousness is born into this world; starts his life through passing time, meets his inheritance and environment, and begins to learn about them and from them.

The result of this process is the formation of a personality and body which is of its very nature disturbed and subject to breakdown. It cannot happen any other way. The Jack Principle, the nature of passing time, the environment and inheritance make it so. The sense of wonder and the ability for direct response without the action of the personality, which are characteristics of childhood are soon covered over, so that a person becomes unable to respond to anything without the interference of his personality.

The personality refers everything to its memory bank of learned responses and judgments. Nothing new gets in without being coloured by old judgments, and only predetermined responses come out. In effect the personality takes over, and answers for the individual, who goes to sleep and becomes part of the subconscious, though this may ultimately rebel if it is not altogether smothered.

Personalities adapt and can be adjusted to situations which upset them, but the whole process is mechanical, so there is only endless change without any real inner growth, and no individual evolution of man can occur. In this way fashions change, technologies rise and fall, cataclysms occur every few millenia, but mankind remains, with very few exceptions, fearful, violent and self-righteous, not knowing why he is here or where he is going.

Applying this general statement to health and disease one can get some idea of how Nature works through time, the environment and inheritance, by comparing a non industrialised agricultural community with little sanitation, no generalised piped water supply and inadequate health care, with an industrialised community with a high standard of sanitation and water supply and more than adequate health care.

The expectancy of life in the former is about 30-40 years, while that of the latter is about 70 years. The deaths in the former are mainly from infectious illnesses and only relatively few from chronic and degenerative disorders. In the latter it is found that deaths from chronic and degenerative disorders predominate and that gradually they spread back into the younger age groups, and that even though technology and medical treatment improve, some new and intractible disorders appear so that the previous rate of improvement in life expectancy is not maintained. There is a high incidence of minor emotional disturbances and chronic ill health.

In Western Europe and the USA we have moved from the first of these communities into the latter during the last 150 years and the available statistics confirm that what is described in the preceding paragraph is now happening[158][142]. It seems that a life expectancy of 30-40 years is not appropriate for man, and when a feudal system is replaced by something more equitable for the whole population, the expectancy of life improves. Yet in tranquil temperate agricultural areas with a stable population, which does not engage in wars continually and keeps working without retirement, such as remote areas in the Andes and Caucasus, the life expectancy may go much higher, even though the plumbing and inhabitants are poor. That is the life which suits man — not the restless wheeler-dealer and commutor factory life governed by the Jack Principle as is now the Western style.

It would be preferable if national statistics were no longer collected under separate headings such as Economics, Death and Disease Rates, Sociology and Religion. An attempt might be made to establish a quality of life index which could be called the Qualife Index, or QI. On the bad side would be a number of morbidity rates which would count as minus values and on the good side a number of happy measurements — such as — such as what? There are not many to record. We do not have ways of measuring well-being and enjoyment except in negative terms. Perhaps one index which might be used is the number of centenarians in possession of their senses who can certify that they enjoy life. It should not be difficult to show rapid improvement in that statistic there are so few of such people, though this was not always so. In ancient India the life expectancy was from 70-116 years, averageing 100[175].

In addition to the usual death rates on the morbid side, a number of factors seem to be worthwhile monitoring such as the rates for the number of working days lost by illness, numbers of pills or tonnage of psychotropic drugs per head of the population, numbers of hospital admissions for overdose of drugs, number of days lost through strikes, the amount of money spent on the armed forces per head of population, number of troops killed in action per year.

number of murders per year, number of bomb explosions per year, number of unemployed, number of battered babies, number of illiterates and so on.

Factorial analysis would soon sort out the value of each component used in the index, and would lead to a number of factors being shown to be unsuitable, while others kept under observation for sometime would be found useful to put into the QI.

## How to Plan a Strategy for Life

It would be better if we did not concentrate on the treatment of disease and its politics, but directed our energies onto finding the reasons why it arises. It is preferable not to concentrate only on avoidance of what has been shown to be inevitable. That activity is just tactics – a temporary escape from a situation which alters the immediate local state, but has no effect on the overall strategic situation.

It is better tactics to avoid an enemy that has superior forces and is bound to win in the end, like passing time, whose manifestations are disease and death, than engage in a struggle with him. But the essential strategic problem is how to avoid being here on Earth in passing time, and therefore subject to disease. We have not been able to avoid getting here. We are here, and from this position we need to escape. How shall we set about it? What is the right strategy? Once we start thinking like this our attitudes to life and death alter – life becomes very valuable – death loses its terror.

Do not spend too much effort trying only to eradicate disease – try to avoid it surely, but when it occurs, discover that it is telling you what must be changed in yourself or your surroundings. Learn from it, to act like that is far more worthwhile than going straight to the mechanical practitioners of mechanical systems and asking them to rid you of the discomfort or disability at any price by unloading your own responsibilities upon them.

The basic strategy of life should be to learn to live in harmony with all men, nature and the cosmos — to make a great aim to transcend one's human nature. Smaller aims on the way towards attaining that aim involve much long effort to overcome one's inherent Jack Principle and become a balanced Human Being who can co-operate with Nature and his fellow men. We are not on Earth to use it up and poop off fireworks, chat with the spirit world, have ecstatic experiences and coerce others or be fanatics. We are here to find our purpose and then to fulfil it. We have only ourselves to contend with.

When enough people practice this strategy of life the need for many methods or therapy or polyactrics[49] as it has been called will be greatly reduced — men will be able to heal themselves, or if not accept their Karma and work it out. They will be beyond the opposites of Health and Disease.

So the first realisation to make is that we are in a trap on earth. Without this one just chunters on at the mercy of one's life, environment and habits of mind. Then one needs to realise that one is responsible for one's fate and can do something about it, and one must want this very much in order to make long and continued efforts to get one's unbalanced and disturbed state right. Putting it now in the terms already mentioned one must become *Conscious* of one's plight, one must make an *Aim* to seek a way to change it and one must have the *Will* to carry out that aim.

If one follows that aim, one looks for people who have gone the same way before, and soon finds their traces. There are teachers and schools everywhere in the world today engaged in such work. There are many books published on the subject. It is only when one begins to search that one finds that what one is seeking has existed in civilisation for thousands of years and is currently present around one unrecognised for what it was, until one made the aim. But not only do aims differ, so do tastes and types. What suits one person will not do for another.

From the wide selection of schools and teachers you should choose what suits you. If one does not appeal, try another. When you find the right one, you will know because it works for you. That is the advice of one teacher[154] talking about the 122 methods of meditation given on the Vigyana Bhairava and Sochanda Tantra[165], which is 5,000 years old.

These are in alphabetical order for there is no difference in merit, only in compatibility:—
Anthroposophy; Arcane School; Baha'i; Buddhism; Christianity, Gurdjieff ("the Work") School; Hinduism; Islam; Ittoen; Jainism; Judaism; Psychosynthesis; Subud; Sufism; Taoism; Theosophy; Transcendental meditation; Zen and others.

When you have found a technique or a system or a teacher which feels right for you, work with your whole energy. Do not expect a sudden enlightenment. These spectacular events are blind alleys. If you seek you cannot find — if you desire you cannot find. Little by little small gifts of understanding arise, but one has to be conscious enough to perceive them. This is what makes life so valuable.

Possibly the way of working you first choose will not remain the right one for you as you grow spiritually. If you truly feel this, change it — find another. You will then soon know whether you were right or wrong. If you were wrong do not be too proud to return.

## Avoid fanaticism

There are several pitfalls here however. In all teachings, the personality is bypassed and it does not like this. So it either denigrates the method, and makes you so unhappy in it that you leave it to try another, or it takes the system over by identifying itself with it. So one becomes a fanatic, only able to see the good of that particular teaching with which the personality is identified, trying to coerce others to it, and getting upset if they do not respond or if they continue to maintain a different point of view.

## The Dangers of Organisation

Another trouble is that around every teacher or method an organisation develops. In his lifetime a strong teacher may be able to stave off the dangerous effects of organisation (chapter 1). But later the integrity of the teaching depends on the arising of other teachers of the same level of enlightenment as the founder, and this, though it does occur, becomes less frequent as time passes. So many ancient and good systems are today run only by fanatics. Much can be learnt from them, but there will come a time in spiritual growth when it will be felt inwardly that it is essential to move on. That is why I believe that most can be understood from living teachers. Khrishnamurti[137] and Rajneesh[154] are two such beings.

The reason for leaving a group or movement may not be the valid one of escaping from the restricting and disordering effect of an organisation run by fanatics, but because inevitably if one is an active type one will some day feel the essential inner need to stand alone and find a way from within oneself. If one is passive one can stay where one is and do the same, both ways have their difficulties, as anyone who has been through the process will discover. On the active path one feels alone — terribly alone; one loses one's way, and has to struggle to maintain the aim. On the passive path one has to keep very quiet not to fall foul of the organisation, and one lives in constant danger of being found out. The resulting dissimulation may have a distressing effect — St. John of the Cross called it the dark night of the soul. However in the end one sees it does not matter, for one has started to become conscious beyond the opposites which dominate the personality.

# References and Bibliography

*The items in heavy type are a suggested bibliography for further reading.*

1. ACLAND, R., *The Next Step.* Published by author, 1975.
2. ALLEN, J. H., *The Chronic Miasms.* Boericke & Tafel, Philadelphia, U.S.A. Out of print, reprinted in India.
3. ASSAGIOLI, R., *The Act of Will.* Wildwood House, London, 1974.
4. ———, *Psychosynthesis.* Viking Compass, 1971.
5. AUDUS, L. J., *Magnetotropism – a new plant growth response.* Nature, 185, 132, 1960.
6. **BAILEY, A. A., *Esoteric Healing.* Lucis Press, London, 1972.**
7. BARBAULT, A., *Gold of a Thousand Mornings.* Spearman, London, 1975.
8. BARBER, T. X., *Physiological Effects of Hypnosis and Suggestion.* Biofeedback and Selfcontrol Annual, Aldine Atherton, New York, 238–9, 1970.
9. BARLOW, W., *The Alexander Principle.* Arrow Books, 1975.
10. BARNOTHY, M. F., Ed., *Biological Effects of Magnetic Fields.* Plenum Press, New York, 1964.
11. BELLHOUSE, E., *Vitaflorum Trust News Letter.* Summer 1973.
12. ———, *Ibid.* Xmas 1974.
13. ———, *Ibid.* Easter 1975.

14. BHATTACHARYYA, B., *Gem Therapy.* Firma K. L. Mukhopadhyay, Calcutta, 1971.

15. ———, *The Science of Cosmic Ray Therapy or Teletherapy.* Firma K. L. Mukhopadhyay, Calcutta, 1972.

16. ———, *Septenate Mixtures in Homoeopathy.* Firma K. L. Mukhopadhyay, 1972.

17. ———, *Magnet Dowsing.* Firma K. L. Mukhopadhyay, 1967.

18. ———, *The Science of Cosmic Ray Therapy or Teletherapy.* Firma K. L. Mukhopadhyay, Calcutta, 1972, p. 82.

19. BIDWELL, R. G. S., *Plant Physiology.* Macmillan, 1974, p. 399.

20. BIOFEEDBACK & SELF-CONTROL ANNUAL. Aldine Atherton, New York.

21. BIRREN, W., *Colour Psychology and Colour Therapy.* University Books, New York, 1961, p. 122.

22. BLAVATSKY, H. P., *Collected Writings,* I, II, V, VI, VII, VIII, IX, X. Theosophical Publishing House, U.S.A., India, London, 1966.

    ———, *The Secret Doctrine,* 2 vols. Theosophical Press, U.S.A., 1952.

    ———, *The Voice of the Silence.* Aquarian Press, 1953.

    ———, *Isis Unveiled,* 2 vols. Theosophical Press, 1972.

23. BLYTHE, P., *Drugless Medicine.* Arthur Barker, London, 1974.

24. BOEHME, J., *Works of, "Law Edition".* 4 vols. London, 1814. and HARTMANN, F., *qv.*

25. BRESTED, I. H., *History of Egypt.* New York, 1909, p. 384.

26. BROWNE, T., *Religio Medici and other writings.* Everyman's Library, Dent, p. 5.

27. BRUNTON, P., *A Search in Secret Egypt.* Arrow Books, 1965, p. 56. 1st edition, Rider, 1935.

28. BURANG, T., *The Tibetan Art of Healing.* Watkins, London, 1974.

29. ———, *Ibid.* p. 17.

30. BURR, H. S., *Blueprint for Immortality: The Electric Patterns of Life.* Neville Spearman, London, 1972.

31. CADE, C. M., and WOOLLEY-HART, A., *Psychochemical studies of Hypnotic Phenomena.* British Journal of Clinical Hypnosis, 5, 14, 1974.

32. CARLSON, R. J., *The Frontiers of Science and Medicine.* Wildwood House, London, 1975, pp. 7–45.

33. CATELL, R. B., EBER, H. W. & TATSUOKA, M. M., *Handbook for the 16 Personality Factor Test.* NFER Publishing Co. Ltd., 1970.

34. CHENG, M. & SMITH, R. W., *T'ai Chi: the 'Supreme Ultimate' exercise for Health, Sport and Self-defence.* Chas. Tuttle, Rutland, Vermont, U.S.A., 1967.

35. CLIFFORD, Jr., J. D., *Degree of Injunction.* Quoted in REICH, W., Selected Writings. *qv.* pp. 540–44.

36. COLLIN, R., *The Theory of Celestial Influence.* Stuart, London, 1954.

37. COOK, T. A., *The Curves of Life: Being an account of Spiral Formations.* London, 1914.

38. DA LIU, *T'ai Chi Chuan and I Ching.* Routledge and Kegan Paul, London, 1974.

39. DAVIS, A. R. & BHATTACHARYYA, A. K., *Magnet & Magnetic Fields or Healing by Magnets.* Firma K. L. Mukhopadhyay, Calcutta, 1970.

40. DAY, L. & DELAWARR, G., *New Worlds beyond the Atom.* Stuart, London, 1956.

41. de LANGRE, J., *The First Book of Do-In.* Happiness Press, California, 1971.

42. ———, *The Second Book of Do-In.* Happiness Press, California, 1974.

43. DUKE, M., *Acupuncture – The Chinese Art of Healing.* Constable, London, 1972.

44. ———, *Ibid.* 158 ff.

45. DUNBAR, F., *Psychosomatic Diagnosis.* Hoeber, New York & London, 1943.

46. EDWARDS, H., *Spirit Healing.* Healer Publishing Co. Ltd., 1960.

47. ELGOOD, C., *Medical History of Persia and the Eastern Caliphate, from the earliest times until A.D. 1932.* Cambridge University Press, 1951, pp. 19–20.

48. ENGEL, G. L., *A Psychological Setting of Somatic Disease: The 'Giving up – Given up' complex.* Proc. Roy. Soc. Med. vol. 60, p. 553, 1966.

49. ERSKINE, D., *Polyatrics.* Delawarr Laboratories Newsletter, Winter 1974.

50. EVANS, M., *Article in 'Work Arising'.* Ed. Davy, J., Rudolf Steiner Press, 1975.

51. EVANS-WENTZ, W. Y., *Tibetan Yoga and Secret Doctrines.* Oxford University Press, 1935.

52. ———, *Ibid.* p. 157.

53. FORBES, A., *Try Being Human.* Langdon Books, 1973.

54. ———, *Ibid.*

55. ———, *Ibid.* pp. 59–62.

56. ———, *Ibid.* Watch Exercise use index.

57. ———, *Ibid.* p. 12.

58. FRANKL, V. E., *The Doctor and the Soul.* Penguin Books, 1973.

59. ———, *Psychotherapy and Existentialism.* Penguin Books, 1973.

**60. GALLERT, M. L., *New Light on Therapeutic Energies.* James Clarke, London, 1966, pp. 175 ff.**

61. ———, *Ibid.* pp. 19–46.

62. ———, *Ibid.* pp. 57–90.

63. GAUQUELIN, M., *The Cosmic Clocks.* Peter Owen & Paladin Books, 1973.

64. ———, *Ibid.* pp. 141–43.

65. GHADIALI, D., Quoted by GALLERT, M. L., in *New Light on Therapeutic Energies,* Clarke, London, 1966, p. 34.

66. GHYKA, M., *Geometrical Composition and Design.* Tiranti, London, 1952.

67. ———, *The Geometry of Art and Life.* Sheed and Ward, 1945.

68. ———, *Ibid.* p. 52.

69. GOVINDA, A., *Foundations of Tibetan Mysticism.* Rider, 1960.

70. ———, *Ibid.* p. 134 & 147 ff.

71. GREEN, E., *Biofeedback for Mind-body Self Regulation and Creativity.* Biofeedback and Self Control Annual, 1972, p. 152.

72. GUIRDHAM, A., *A Foot in both Worlds: a Doctor's autobiography of Psychic Experience.* Neville Spearman, 1974.

**73. GURDJIEFF, G. I., *All and Everything,* 1st series. Routledge and Kegan Paul, 1950.**

74. ———, *Ibid.* Chapters 40 & 41.

75. ———, *Ibid.* p. 750 ff.

76. ———, *Meetings with Remarkable Men,* 2nd series. Routledge and Kegan Paul, 1963.

77. ———, *Life is Real Only when 'I Am',* 3rd series. Triangle Editions, New York, 1975.

78. HAMBIDGE, J., *Dynamic Symmetry in Composition.* Yale University Press, New Haven, U.S.A., 1948.

**79. HAHNEMANN, S., *The Organon of Medicine,* fifth edition, plus alterations and additions. Roy Pub. House, Calcutta, 1961.**

80. HARTMANN, F., *Occult Science in Medicine.* Thorsons, 1898 & 1975.

81. ———, *Ibid.* p. 88.

82. ———, *Ibid.* Preface.

83. ———, *The Life of Paracelsus.* Kegan Paul, 1896.

84. ———, *Personal Christianity – The Doctrines of Jacob Boehme.* F. Ungar Publishing Co., New York & Constable & Co., London.

85. ———, *The Life of Paracelsus.* Kegan Paul, 1896.
86. ———, *Ibid.* Use index.
87. **HAUSCHKA, R., *The Nature of Substance.* Stuart, London, 1966.**
88. HOPKINS, E. W., *Religions of India.* London, 1896, p. 559.
89. HORN, J. S., *Away with all Pests.* Hamlyn, 1969, pp. 73–4.
90. ———, *Ibid.* pp. 70–80.
91. ———, *Ibid.* pp. 36–37.
92. HUNT, R., *The Seven Keys to Colour Healing.* C. W. Daniel & Co. Ltd., 1971.
93. HYDE, F. F., *Therapeutic Use of Herbal Remedies.* New Herbal Practitioner, 1, 19–33, 1974.
94. IAMBLICHUS, *Life of Pythagoras.* Translated by Thomas Taylor. Watkins, London, 1926.
95. ILLICH, I., *Medical Nemesis: The Expropriation of Health.* Calder and Boyars, London, 1975.
96. INGLIS, B., *Fringe Medicine.* Faber & Faber, 1964, pp. 96–97.
97. ———, *Ibid.* pp. 161–2.
98. ———, *Ibid.* pp. 199–208.
99. **ISAACS, J. M. A., *Healing in the Context of Psychic Phenomena.* Journal of Brit. Soc. of Dowsers, vol. xxv, no. 5, p. 2, 1975.**
100. JACK, R. A. F., *Introducing Homoeopathy into General Practice.* Published by Nelson & Co. Ltd., 73 Duke Street, London W.1.
101. JENNY, H., *Cymatics.* Basileus Press, Basel, Switzerland, 1966.
102. ———, *Visualising Sound.* Science Journal, June, 1968.
103. JONES, W., *Discourses delivered before the Asiatic Society, and miscellaneous papers on religion, poetry and literature,* 2 vols. London, 1821, reissued 1824.
104. JUNG, C. J., *Psychology and Alchemy.* Vol. 12 of Collected Works. Routledge and Kegan Paul, 1953.
105. ———, *Mysterium Conjunctionis.* Vol. 14 of Collected Works. Routledge and Kegan Paul, 1963.

106. KANDINSKY, W., *The Art of Spiritual Harmony*, translated with an introduction by M. T. H. Sadler. Constable, London, 1914.

107. KARAGULLA, S., *Breakthrough to Creativity*. De Vorss and Co., Los Angeles, California, U.S.A., 1967.

108. KAYSER, H., *Harmonia Plantarium*. B. Schwabe and Co., Basel, 1943.

109. KOLISKO, L., *Spirit in Matter*. Kolisko Archive, Stroud, 1948.

110. KOLOSIMO, P., *Not of this World*. Sphere Books, 1971.

111. KUNZANG, J., *Tibetan Medicine*. The Wellcome Institution, 1973.

112. ———, *Ibid.* pp. 38 & 104 ff.

113. KUTUMBIAH, P., *Ancient Indian Medicine*. Orient Longmans, 1962 & 1969.

114. ———, *Ibid.* pp. iii and xliii.

115. ———. *Ibid.* p. xli.

116. ———, *Ibid.* p. 76.

117. ———, *Ibid.* p. 80.

118. LANDAU, R., *God is my Adventure*. Nicholson and Watson, 1935.

119. LAWSON-WOOD, D. & J., *Acupuncture Handbook*. Health Science Press, 1973.

120. ———, *Five Elements of Acupuncture and Chinese Massage*. Health Science Press, 1973.

121. ———, *First Aid at your Finger Tips*. Health Science Press, 1963.

122. LEAKE, C. D., LARKEY, S. V. & LUTZ, H. F., *Science, Medicine and History*. Oxford.

123. **LEADBEATER, C. W., *Man Visible and Invisible*, first published 1902. Quest Book edition, Theosophical Publishing House, Wheaton, Illinois, U.S.A., 1969.**

124. LE CORBUSIER, *The Modulor*. Faber and Faber, 1961.

125. **LE SHAN, L., *The Medium, the Mystic and the Physicist*. Turnstone Books, 1974, pp. 197–217.**

126. ———, *Ibid.* pp. 99–140.

127. LIANG, T. T., *T'ai Chi Ch'uan for Health and Self-Defense*. Redwing Book Co., Boston, U.S.A., 1974.

**128. LILLY, J. C., *In the Centre of the Cyclone*. Paladin Books, 1973.**

129. ———, *Ibid*. p. 28.

130. LINDEMANN, H., *Relieve Tension the Autogenic Way*. Abelard-Schumann, London, 1974.

131. LONG, M. F., *The Secret Science behind Miracles*. Huna Research Publications, 1948.

132. ———, *The Secret Science at Work*. Huna Research Publications, 1953.

133. ———, *The Huna Code in Religions*. Huna Research Publications, 1965.

134. LUSCHER, M., translated by Scott, I., *The Luscher Colour Test*. Jonathan Cape, London, 1970.

135. LUTHE, W., *Autogenic Training*. Vols. I–VI. Grune and Stratton, New York, 1969–1973.

136. ———, *Autogenic Therapy: Excerpts on Applications to Cardiovascular Disorders and Hypercholesteraemia*. Biofeedback & Self Control Annual, 1971, p. 437.

137. LUTYENS, M., *The Penguin Krishnamurti Reader*. Penguin Books, London, 1970.

138. MANN, F., *Acupuncture: The Ancient Chinese Art of Healing*. Heinemann, London, 1962.

139. MOTOYAMA, H., *Do Meridians (Keiraku) exist, and what are they like?* Research for Religion & Parapsychology, Tokyo, Japan, Vol. 1, No. 1; 1–48, 1975.

140. ———, *How to measure and diagnose the functions of Meridians*. *Ibid*. Vol. 1, No. 2, 1–29, Sept. 1975.

141. NEW YORK TIMES. News Service. 26 August 1975.

**142. OFFICE OF HEALTH ECONOMICS, *No. 21, Disorders which shorten Life*. London, Nov. 1966.**

143. OGATA, S., *Zen for the West*. Rider, London, 1959.

144. OHSAWA, G., *Acupuncture and the Philosophy of the Far East.* Tao Publications Inc., Boston, 1973.

**145. OSTRANDER, S. & SCHROEDER, L.,** ***PSI: Psychic Discoveries behind the Iron Curtain.*** **Abacus, London, 1970, pp. 358–389.**

146. OUSPENSKY, P. D., *In Search of the Miraculous.* Routledge & Kegan Paul, London, 1950. Use Index.

147. ———, *The Psychology of Man's Possible Evolution.* Hodder and Stoughton, London, 1951. Use Index.

148. PACHTER, H. M., *Paracelsus: Magic into Science.* Schumann, New York, 1951. Use Index.

149. PALOS, S., *The Chinese Art of Healing.* Bantam Books, New York, 1972.

150. PARCHMENT, S. R., *Astrology Mundane and Spiritual.* Rosicrucian Anthroposophical League, California, 1933, pp. 540–621.

151. PAUL, ST., New Testament, Revised Standard Version. 1 Cor. Chapters 12–14.

152. PIERREAKOS, J. C., *The Energy Field in Man and Nature.* Institute of Bioenergetic Analysis, New York, 1971.

153. RAE, M., *Potency-simulation by Magnetically Energised Patterns.* Radionic Quarterly, March 1973.

154. RAJNEESH, *The Book of Secrets,* Vols. 1–5. Rajneesh Foundation Publications, Poona, 1974.

155. RAMACHARAKA, Yogi, *The Science of Psychic Healing.* Fowler, London, 1968.

156. ———, *The Science of Breath.* Fowler, London, 1960.

157. RAWSON, D. S., *Science and Homoeopathy.* The Hahnemannian Gleanings, Vol. XL, August, 1973.

158. REGISTRAR GENERAL, *Decennial Supplement, England and Wales, 1961. Occupational Mortality Tables.* H.M.S.O., London, 1971.

159. REICH, W., *The Function of the Orgasm.* Panther Books, London, 1961.

160. ———, *Selected Writings*. Farrar, Strauss & Giroux, 1973, pp. 183–446.

161. ———, *The Mass Psychology of Fascism*. Penguin Books, 1975.

162. ———, *The Invasion of Compulsory Sex-Morality*. Penguin Books, 1975.

163. ———, *Reich Speaks of Freud*. Penguin Books, 1975.

164. ———, *Listen Little Man*. Penguin Books, 1975, p. 90.

165. REPS, P., *Zen Flesh, Zen Bones*. Penguin Books, 1971, p. 151.

166. REYNER, J. H., (In collaboration with Lawrence, G. & Upton, C.) *Psionic Medicine*. Routledge & Kegan Paul, London, 1974.

167. RHAGADAN, V., *Indian Medicine in the Classical Age*. Chowkhamba Sanscrit Series Office, 1972, p. 14.

168. RICHARDS, W. G., *The Chain of Life*. L. J. Speight Ltd., Bradford, Devon, 1954, pp. 6 ff.

169. ———, *Ibid*. All.

170. SARKAR, B. K., Forward to HAHNEMANN, *Organon of Medicine*. qv. 1961, pp. VII & IX.

171. SCHINDLER, M., *Goethe's Theory of Colour*. New Knowledge Books, London, 1964.

172. SEMEONOFF, B., Ed., *Personality Assessment, Selected Readings*. Penguin Books, 1966.

173. SHARMA, C. H., *A Manual of Homoeopathy and Natural Medicine*. Turnstone, London, 1975.

174. ———, *A Plea for a New Medicine*. Radionic Quarterly, Vol. 20, 18–28, June, 1974.

175. SHARMA, P. V., *Indian Medicine in the Classical Age*. Chowkhamba Sanscrit Series Office, Varanasi 1, 1972, p. 27.

176. SIERRA, R. U., *Biomagnetics and Healing*. Human Dimensions, Vol. 13, no. 1, p. 31, 1974.

177. SMITH, J., *The Influence of Enzyme Growth by the 'Laying on of Hands'*. The Dimensions of Healing Symposium, Stanford University Press, California, 1972, p. 110.

178. ———, *Ibid.* p. 112.

179. SPEIGHT, P., *A Comparison of the Chronic Miasms.* Health Science Press, 1961.

**180. STEINER, R., *The Anthroposophical Approach to Medicine.* Anthroposophical Publishing Co., London, 1928, p. 26.**

181. ———, *The Story of My Life.* Anthroposophical Pub. Co., 1928.

182. ———, *The Anthroposophical Approach to Medicine.* Anthroposophical Pub. Co., London, 1928, pp. 11 & 12.

183. STEINER, R. & WEGMAN, I., *The Fundamentals of Therapy.* Anthroposophical Press, London, 1925, p. 3.

184. STEINER, R., *The Anthroposophical Approach to Medicine.* Anthroposophical Pub. Co., London, 1928, pp. 14 & 15.

185. ———, *Spiritual Science and Medicine.* R. Steiner Pub. Co., London, 1948, pp. 82–108.

186. ———, *Ibid.* pp. 70–71.

187. ———, *Ibid.* pp. 135–136.

188. ———, *Problems of Nutrition.* Anthr. Press Inc., New York, 1969.

189. ———, *Spiritual Science and Medicine.* R. Steiner Pub. Co., London, 1948, pp. 136–138.

190. STEINER, R. & WEGMAN, I., *The Fundamentals of Therapy.* Anthr. Press, London, 1925.

191. STEINER, R., *Illusory Illness and the Feverish Pursuit of Health.* Anthrop. Press, New York, 1969, p. 21.

192. ———, *The Manifestations of Karma.* R. Steiner Pub. Co., London, 1947.

193. SUZUKI, D. T., *An Introduction to Zen Buddhism.* Rider, London, 1948.

194. TANSLEY, D., *Radionics and the Subtle Anatomy of Man.* Health Science Press, 1972.

195. ———, *Radionics – Interface with the Ether Fields.* Health Science Press, 1975.

196. THAKKUR, C. G., *Introduction to Ayurveda.* Ancient Wisdom Publications, Bombay, 1965, p. xviii.

197. ———, *Ibid.* pp. 46 & 47.

198. ———, *Ibid.* p. 3.

199. ———, *Ibid.* p. 129.

200. ———, *Ibid.* p. 134.

201. ———, *Ibid.* p. 111.

202. THEOSOPHICAL RESEARCH CENTRE, LONDON, *Some unrecognised Factors in Medicine.* Theosophical Publishing House, London, 1939.

203. THOMAS, Trans, GIULLAMONT, A., et al., *The Gospel according to Thomas.* Collins, London, 1959, p. 53.

204. THOMPSON, D'A., *On Growth and Form.* Cambridge, 1942.

205. THOMSON, C. L., *The Naturopathic Approach.* The Kingston Chronicle, Nov. 1971.

206. TOMAS, A., *We are not the First.* Sphere Books, 1972.

**207. TOMPKINS, P. & BIRD, C., *The Secret Life of Plants.* Penguin Books, 1975.**

208. ———, ———, *Ibid.* p. 146.

**209. TROMP, S. W., *Psychical Physics.* Elsevier Pub. Co., U.S.A., 1949, pp. 211–213, 264–282, 344–349.**

210. VEITH, I., trans., *The Yellow Emperor's Classic of Internal Medicine.* Univ. of California Press, 1966.

211. ———, *Ibid.* p. 3.

**212. WACHSMUTH, G., *The Etheric Formative Forces in Cosmos, Earth & Man.* Anthr. Pub. Co., London, 1932.**

213. ———, *Ibid.* p. 144.

214. ———, *Ibid.* pp. 144–147.

215. WANG, C. Y., *The Mental Elucidation of the Thirteen Postures.* Trans. by LIANG, T. T. *qv.* p. 17.

216. WALLACE, R. K., *The Physiological Effects of Transcendental*

*Meditation*. Biofeedback and Self Control Annual. Aldine-Atherton, New York, 1970, pp. 107 & 109.

217. ———, BENSON, H. & WILSON, A. F., *A Wakeful Hypometabolic Physiological State. Ibid.* 1971, pp. 142–143.

218. WARREN, S., *A Compendium of the Theological Writings of Emmanuel Swedenborg*. Swedenborg Society, 1901.

219. WATSON, L., *Is Primitive Medicine really Primitive?* May Lectures 1974 in The Frontiers of Science and Medicine, pp. 69–83, edited by CARLSON, R. J. Wildwood House, London, 1975.

**220.** ———, ***Supernature*. Hodder and Stoughton, London, 1973.**

221. ———, *Ibid.* pp. 90–106.

222. WATTS, A. W., *The Way of Zen*. Thames and Hudson, 1957.

223. WEEKS, N., *The Medical Discoveries of Edward Bach, Physician*. C. W. Daniel Co. Ltd., 1940.

224. WEIL, A. W., *The Natural Mind*. Jonathan Cape, London, 1973.

**225. WESTLAKE, A. T., *The Pattern of Health*. Stuart, London, 1961 and Shambala, U.S.A., 1974.**

226. ———, *Ibid.* pp. 39–46.

227. WHALLEY, W. B., *Annual Scientific Lecture at the Royal College of Physicians*. 4th Dec. 1974 in World Medicine.

228. WHITMAN, J., *The Psychic Power of Plants*. Star Books, 1975.

229. ———, *Ibid.*

230. WICKES, F. G., *The Inner World of Man*. Methuen, London, 1950.

231. WILCOX, J., *Radionics and Psychoenergetics*. Radionic Quarterly, Vol. 21, no. 4, 1975.

232. WILHELM, R., *The Secret of the Golden Flower*. Routledge and Kegan Paul, London, 1931.

233. WILSON, C., *Wilhelm Reich*. The Village Press, London, 1974.

234. WOOD, E., *Yoga*. Penguin Books, London, 1959.

235. WORLD MEDICINE EDITORIAL, World Medicine, 26 March 1975.

236. WU Wei-P'ing, *Chinese Acupuncture*. Health Science Press, 1962.

237. ———, *Ibid.* pp. 13–15.

# Index

Activity, displacement, 8
Acupuncture, 14-18, 39, 93, 97, 100, 115, 139, 146, 147
Agpao, Tony, 49
Alchemy, 2, 122
Alcohol, 8, 162
Alexander method, 37-8, 41
Allergy, 34, 36, 131
Allopathy, 3, 4, 9, 19-23, 29, 32, 55, 58, 64-5, 72, 92, 101, 108, 114, 118, 138, 147, 151
American Indian, 2
Anaemia, 20
Anthroposophy, 24-31, 108, 132, 169
Antimitotics, 20
Antidepressants, 20
Anxiety, 20, 131, 158
Arcane school, 124, 169
Aroma therapy, 2
Arthritis, 17, 84, 131
Ash, Dr M., 139
Asthma, 34, 36, 70, 131
Astral body, 25
Astrology, 26, 53, 83, 160-1
Atheroma, 84, 118, 157, 158, 162
Autogenic Training, 71, 129-31
Autosuggestion, 129
Axham Dr F., 12
Ayurveda, 54, 58, 74, 78, 98, 100-9, 118

Bach remedies, 66-9, 80, 84, 89
Baha'i, 169
Bailey, Alice, 52
Behaviour therapy, 37, 69, 123
Being 142, 168
Belief, 46, 141
Bhagavad Gita, 39
Bhattacharyya B., 74, 78, 83, 108
Biofeedback, 69-72, 132
Birren W., 72, 75
Blood, 138
— , pressure, 69
Body, physical, 9, 10, 25, 108
— , supraphysical, 1, 25, 108, 120-121
Boehme J., 24, 55
Bonesetters, 33, 114
Bonghan corpuscles, 15

Brain, 27
— , waves, 69, 132
Brested I.H., 77
Breathing, 40
Broadcasting, 74, 138
Browne, Sir T., 42
Buddhism, 51, 99, 100, 154, 169
Business combines, 6

Cancer, 20, 84, 87-8, 94, 118
Care, health, 8, 51
Cataract, 48
Centre, 42
Chakras, 1, 138
Charity, negative, 7
Ch'i, 15, 40, 72, 77, 84, 109
Chiropractic, 32-6, 41, 93, 115, 145, 146, 147, 148
Chladni E.G., 76, 78
Choice, 152
Christianity, 169
Christian Science, 47, 131-2
Church, 48, 50, 150, 163
Clairvoyancy, 45, 121, 144
Colds, 92, 131
Colour, 29, 72-5, 81, 84, 108, 138
Consciousness, 28, 124-5
Cooking, 29, 113
Coronary disease, 131, 157
Cosmos, 25, 28, 29, 158
Counselling, 124
Cramp, 17
Culpepper T., 53-4
Cycles, 82-3, 153
Cymatics, 55, 75-82, 103, 138, 139

Death, 1, 150, 154, 156, 158, 159, 167
Defences, psychological, 11
Depression, 20, 68, 123, 158
Determined, other, 7
— , self, 7
Diet, 27, 56, 93, 95, 113, 118, 161
Digestion, 14, 113-4
Diminishing returns, 142-3
Disease, 28, 103, 132, 142, 157-8, 160-4
— , iatrogenic, 5, 27
— , chronic, 20, 66, 93
Displacement activity, 8

Doctors, 2, 4, 9, 10, 51, 56, 62, 63, 99, 123, 150
Do-in, 51, 115
Dowsing, 133-7, 144-5
Drown, Ruth, 12, 138
Drugs, 122-3, 162
— , side effects, 5, 21

ECT, 123
Ectoderm, 14
Education, 71
Edwards, Harry, 47
E.E.C., 4, 65, 150-1
Effects, side, 5, 27
Egypt, 72, 77, 78, 96
Electrocardiogram, 70
Electroencephalogram, 128, 132
Emotions, 68, 104, 155, 159-60
— , negative, 11, 156, 165
Endoderm, 14
Energy, 14, 44, 87
Environment, 160
Epilepsy, 69
Ether, 77, 103
Etheric body, 25
Exaltation of Flowers, 2
Experimental method, 2

Faith, 46, 155
Fanaticism, 155, 170
Fear, 6, 68, 123, 126, 156
Feeling, 10, 159-60
Fields, 75, 144-5
Fits, 69, 123
Flowers, 67, 89, 132
Food, 29, 113-4, 152, 161
Force, 87, 103
Form, 78-82
Fractures, 114
Frankl, V., 126

Gallert, M., 36, 73, 87
Gauquelin, M., 54, 83
Gem therapy, 72-5
General Medical Council, 22, 68, 146, 150
Ghadiali, D., 73
Ghandi, 54
Ghyka, M., 79
Goethe, W., 75
Golden mean, 79
Gravity, 137
Growth, 78-9, 84, 85, 91, 157, 160
Guirdham, Dr A., 46
Gurdjieff, G.I., 31, 78, 111, 124, 133, 154, 169

Hahnemann, S., 58-60, 63, 64, 66, 69, 145
Hambidge, J., 79
Hand diagnosis, 2
— healing, 44, 75, 115
Hartmann, Dr F., 4, 13

Hatha yoga, 39, 41
Headache, 29, 36
Healing, 32, 43-52, 56, 72, 82, 106, 117, 139, 141, 146
— , hand, 44, 75, 115
— , psychic, 48, 116
— , spirit, 44-5, 116, 141
Health, 132, 146, 157
— , care, 8, 151
Heart, 70, 114
— , disease, 131
Heilpraktiker, 147
Hepatitis, 17
Herbalism, 26, 53-7, 83, 93, 147
Hindu, 84, 97, 154, 169
Hippocrates, 19, 58
Homoeopathy, 18, 20, 26, 55, 56, 58-65, 66, 68, 74, 80, 84, 90, 92, 93, 101, 106, 108, 138-40, 145-7, 163
Huna, 43, 45, 145
Hunt, R., 74
Hubris, 5
Hydrotherapy, 92-3
Hyperchondria, 158
Hypertension, 130, 158
Hypnosis, 127-9

Iatrogenic disease, 5, 27
Illich, I., 4, 5, 6, 12
Immunisation, 20, 59
Impact therapy, 2
Infections, 23, 92, 165
Inheritance, 163
Inner world, 10
Instinct, 129
Institute of Directors, 149
Intuition, 46
Iris diagnosis, 2, 112
Islam, 169
Ittoen, 169

Jack principle, 7, 45, 90, 100, 124, 153, 155, 156, 157, 161, 164, 166, 168
Jainism, 169
Jaundice, 17
Jenny H., 76, 78
Job feeling, 9
Judaism, 169
Jung, Dr C.G., 122, 126

Kahunas, 43
Kandinsky, W., 75
Karma, 133, 163-4
Ki, 15, 39, 40, 44, 51, 72, 77, 84, 109, 116
Krishnamurti, 170
Kushi, M., 111-2, 117
Kunzang, J., 119

Learning, 142
Le Shan, Dr L., 13, 52
Leucotomy, 123

Life, 1, 109, 117, 132, 144, 152, 154, 155, 158, 167
— , expectancy, 165-6
Lilly, Dr J., 42
Lourdes, 47, 49
Lungs, 28, 129
Luscher personality test, 75

Magnetism, 19, 55, 74, 82-5, 137
Mahabhabarata, 19, 42, 84, 160
Man, 142, 152
Manark preparations, 2
Manipulation, 34-5
Mantra, 76, 78, 106, 117
Massage, 29, 35, 93
Materialism, 144
Matter, 19, 84, 90
Medical, profession, 2, 48, 65, 142-4, 150
— , Register, 22
Medicine, 4, 5, 21, 142, 151
— , Act, 1968, 147
Meditation, 30, 69, 132-4
— , Transcendental, 71, 133-4, 169
Mediums, 45
Megavitamins, 2
Mental state, 10
Meridians, 15
Mesoderm, 14
Metabolism, 28
Metals, 26, 106-7
Method, experimental, 2
— , scientific, 151
Mexican Indian, 2
Miasms, 63, 64, 145
Migraine, 36, 70
Mind, 19, 129
Molecule, giant, 59, 60
Motoyama, Dr H., 16
Mortality, 165-66
Moving, 28
Moxa, 16, 115
Muscles, 69, 70

Narcotics, 162
Nation, 6
National Health Service, 18, 51, 57, 62, 143, 144, 147, 151
Nature, 152
Naturopathy, 65, 92-5
Negative charity, 7
Neoplasm, 20, 84, 87-8, 94, 118
Nerves, 14, 27, 33

Obesity, 158, 162
OM, 76
Organisation, 6, 142, 170
Orgone, 85-9
Opposites, 8, 9, 132
Oriental therapy, 31, 32, 33, 39, 40, 93, 96-121

Ohsawa, G., 110, 111
Osteopathy, 32-6, 41, 65, 93, 115, 145, 146, 147, 148
Other determined, 7
Ouija board, 45
Ouspensky P.D., 111

Pain, 8, 20, 159
— , referred, 33
Palmer, D., 33
Paracelsus, 26, 54, 55, 58, 82, 122
Patanjali, 39
Pattern, 55, 59, 60, 68, 80
Pendulum, 16, 108, 135-6, 145
Personality, 6, 164
Pharmacopoeia, British, 53
— , Homoeopathic, 63-4
Pharmaceutical industry, 56, 62, 107, 143
Pills, 21
Plants, 28, 53-5, 78, 84, 85
Potency, 59, 60, 61, 67
Practitioners, 141
— , medical, 56
Prana, 39, 40, 44, 51, 72, 77, 84
Principle, Jack, 7, 45, 90, 100, 124, 153, 155, 156, 157, 161, 164, 166, 168
Problems, 5
Professions, 6
Psionic, medicine, 135, 148
Psychiatry, 122-3, 134
Psychic, healing, 48, 116
— , phenomena, 69
— , surgery, 48
Psychokinesis, 141
Psychology, 120-134
Psychosomatic, 28, 131, 145
Psychosynthesis, 126, 131, 169
Psychotherapy, 20, 123-27, 134, 146
Pulse, 112
Pyonex Treatment, 2

Radiation, 19, 136, 144-5, 162
Radiesthesia, 16, 56, 64, 74, 80, 82, 108, 135-40, 145, 147
Radionics, 65, 80, 135, 140, 146, 148
Rae, M., 80, 139
Rajneesh, 170
Rauwolfia, 54
Reich, W., 12, 85-9, 156
Relativity, 2
Relaxation, 69, 130
Reproduction, 28
Reserpine, 54
Resonance, 103, 136
Returns, diminishing, 142
Rhythm, 28, 129
Rolf, Ida, 38
Rolfing, 38, 41

Schussler's Salts, 2

Science, 2, 10, 11, 13, 25, 45, 120-1
Scientific method, 151
Self, higher, 44
Self love, 7
Senses, 27
Sex, 14, 28, 85, 89, 104, 107, 131
Shiatsu, 17, 51, 115
Side effects, 5
Skin resistance, 128-9
Smith, Sr J., 60, 85
Social conditions, 23, 161
Sorcery, 12
Sound, 76-8, 110
Spine, 34, 35, 37-8, 40-1
Spiral, 14-15, 110
Spirit, 24, 25, 44, 117
Spirits, discarnate, 44-5
Stars, 26
Steiner, R., 13, 15, 24-7, 29-31, 55, 77, 90, 103, 109, 111, 154
Still Dr A., 33
Strategy, 6, 152-171
Stress, 160
Stroke, 70
Subud, 124, 169
Sufi, 124, 133, 154, 169
Surgery, 20, 21, 93, 114
— , psychic, 48
Swedenborg, E., 45
Sydenhamm Sir T., 58
Symptoms, 28, 55, 60
Synergism, 54
Systems, 141

T'ai Chi, 31, 40-2, 115
Tansley, D., 74, 138
Tantra, 154
Taoism, 169
Technology, 10

Temperature control, 72
Tension, 158
Theosophy, 25, 84, 169
Therapy, Far Eastern, 108-18
Thought, 28, 44
Tibetan Therapy, 119-121
Time, 154, 160
Tranquillisers, 20
Transcending, 153
Treatment, 9
Tromp, Dr S.W., 83

Ulcers, peptic, 131
Unani, 2

Vegetarianism, 27
Vita Florum, 84, 89-91
Vitamins 20, 56, 69, 93

Wachsmuth, C., 73, 77
Watch exercise, 71, 127
Water, 59
— , divining, 135, 144-5
Weleda, 30
Westlake, Dr A., 55, 80, 87
Will, 27-8
Witch doctoring, African, 2
Witness for patient, 138, 140
World, inner, 10

Yin-Yang, 83, 105, 109-10, 115
Yoga, 25, 31, 39, 40, 71, 106, 113, 120, 122, 124, 133
— , mantra, 76
— , sutras of Patanjali, 39

Zen, 84, 99, 100, 133, 169
Zone Therapy, 2